THE HISTORIC FAITH

THE HISTORIC FAITH:

SHORT LECTURES

ON

THE APOSTLES' CREED

BROOKE FOSS WESTCOTT, D.D., D.C.L.,

SIXTH EDITION.

Wipf & Stock
PUBLISHERS
Eugene, Oregon

First Edition March 1883.
Second Edition Nov. 1883. *Third Edition* 1885.
Fourth Edition 1890. *Fifth Edition* 1893.
Sixth Edition 1900.

Wipf and Stock Publishers
199 West 8th Avenue, Suite 3
Eugene, Oregon 97401

The Historic Faith
Short Lectures on the Apostles' Creed
By Westcott, B.F.
ISBN: 1-59244-513-6
Publication date 1/29/2004
Previously published by Macmillan and Co., 1900

PREFACE.

THE following Lectures, with the exception of the last, were delivered in the course of my residence at Peterborough in the Summer of 1880. They are now published in fulfilment of a promise made to some who heard them. It was my object to shew the direct bearing of the different articles of our Historic Faith upon our view of the world and of life. For this purpose the form of devotional instruction has many advantages. In this kind of teaching it is impossible to forget the practical issues of belief. The loftiest thoughts necessarily assume the character of motives or guides to action. There is no fear lest the Creed should appear to be merely a collection of propositions leading to certain intellectual consequences. It is felt to be the inspiration of duty. The facts of the Divine Life reach with a present force to all life: they reach to our life.

I have assumed as the basis of my exposition that the Creed is accepted as true in the full form which is current in the Western Church. These things, I presuppose, we believe; it remains to consider the present meaning and effects of our belief. Starting therefore from the familiar text I have endeavoured to determine the relations of the different sections of the Creed to one another, and the significance of the separate clauses. In doing this I have sought to meet the wants of those who without technical knowledge are willing to give to the great problems of life which the Creed illuminates that careful and sustained thought which their paramount importance demands. To settle them by a peremptory effort is to sacrifice the blessing of mental discipline and the growing strength which comes from the realised consciousness that the first Gospel has an answer to our latest questionings.

But while I have had in view a popular treatment of the subject I trust that anyone who wishes to follow out in detail the topics which are touched upon will find that the arrangement which has been followed will give a convenient outline for study. For the sake of such readers I have added a few notes which deal with some points more fully than the limits of the Lectures allowed, and also suggest some lines of inquiry which my experience has shewn me to be fruitful.

There can be little doubt that the Apostles' Creed in its main substance represents the Baptismal Confession of the middle of the second century. But as such it assumes the fact of communion with the Christian Body. It does not therefore contain any articles in regard to the Institutions through which the divine facts set forth in it are brought home to men. The doctrine of the Sacraments and the doctrine of Church organization are implied as matters of experience, and not formulated. The fulness of the life of the Society is recognised as flowing from the Holy Spirit, but nothing is defined as to the exact modes of His operation.

There is an equal absence from the Creed of all statements of abstract dogma. Nothing that is subjective finds a place in it. It is silent on the theory of justification. It has not even received as an addition the key-word of the Council of Nicæa, 'of one substance (essence) with the Father,' which later controversies made necessary for the interpretation of the Faith.

On both grounds it is impossible that the Apostles' Creed should supersede the special Confessions of particular Christian societies, while it underlies them. But though it cannot be taken in itself as a complete expression of what we hold in regard to the facts of our Faith, it brings before us those facts in their simple majesty, and encourages us day by day to bring our interpretations of them to the test of the whole historic Gospel for the guidance of our own lives. The same abstract statements cannot always convey the same meaning.

Each age, each Church, each believer, will indeed read in the record of the historic Creed of Christendom a peculiar message. We learn its power by listening to its message to ourselves. The voice which we can hear now has been made audible to us first; and answering to this is the special work which is committed to our accomplishment.

It has been my desire to indicate what seem to me to be our obligations in asserting and extending the claims of the Faith, as calling to its service not one class of virtues or one type of character or one type of work, but all virtues, all characters and all works in the fulness of their distinctive energies, and according to the forms of their most effective operation. Looking with open eyes upon the facts which we believe and upon the manifold life in which they have been embodied through the ages, with due regard to the authority of the Society and the adequate fulfilment, by the Spirit's help, of his personal duty, 'let each man be fully convinced in his own mind' and bring the offering of himself to GOD. Meanwhile if any thought which is suggested here is allowed to make more clear the living force with which our Faith deals with the doubts, the difficulties, the speculations, the hopes of to-day; to inspire one fellow-worker with a new confidence in maintaining a conflict where each victory must disclose fresh fields to conquer; to suggest that more than one controversy which troubles and divides us turns on topics which we have no faculties to discuss: that will be a full reward for anxious reflection. No one, I think, would venture to speak on such things, unless he looked back to the charge which has been committed to him.

If our prayers need the purifying grace of the Spirit, what shall we say of our attempts to set forth the mysteries—the revelations—of the Gospel? *Brethren, pray for us.*

B. F. W.

BRAEMAR,
Sept. 23, 1882.

NOTICE TO THE SECOND EDITION.

This edition is simply a reprint of the former one with a few corrections of misprints which have been brought to my notice by the kindness of friends.

The welcome which the book has received requires the expression of deep thankfulness; for the welcome is due to the general spirit in which the book is written. And I cannot doubt that the patient study of our 'Historic Faith' in the light of Holy Scripture and of our actual experience, while we believe that the Spirit of GOD still speaks directly to us through the records of the past and through the present facts of life, will bring that confidence of peace in which our work can be accomplished. The promise is for us: *In your patience ye shall win your souls.*

B. F. W.

CAMBRIDGE,
Oct. 26, 1883.

NOTICE TO THE THIRD EDITION.

I have carefully reconsidered these Lectures in the light of criticisms which I have received. Some expressions which have been misinterpreted I have modified, but I have not made any more considerable changes. Fresh study and experience convince me that the lines of thought which I have endeavoured to indicate converge towards that Truth which can alone make us free.

B. F. W.

CAMBRIDGE,
Sept. 30, 1885.

NOTICE TO THE FOURTH EDITION.

In this edition I have added the original texts of the Creeds of Nicæa and Constantinople together with the typical Latin representatives of the latter Creed. Otherwise, with the exception of a few additional references, this edition is a reprint of the last.

B. F. W.

CAMBRIDGE,
Jan. 24, 1890.

Accepistis et reddidistis quod animo et corde semper retinere debetis, quod in stratis vestris dicatis, quod in plateis cogitetis, et quod inter cibos non obliviscamini; in quo etiam dormientes corpore corde vigiletis.

Commemora fidem tuam, inspice te: sit tanquam speculum tibi Symbolum tuum. Ibi te vide, si credis omnia quæ te credere confiteris, et gaude quotidie in fide tua. Sint divitiæ tuæ, sint quotidiana ista quódammodo indumenta mentis tuæ.

AUGUSTINUS.

CONTENTS.

I.

FAITH.

II.

CREEDS.

III.

I BELIEVE IN GOD THE FATHER, ALMIGHTY, MAKER OF HEAVEN AND EARTH.

IV.

AND IN JESUS CHRIST HIS ONLY SON OUR LORD.

V.

WHO WAS CONCEIVED BY THE HOLY GHOST, BORN OF THE VIRGIN MARY, SUFFERED UNDER PONTIUS PILATE, WAS CRUCIFIED, DEAD, AND BURIED.

VI.

HE DESCENDED INTO HELL; THE THIRD DAY HE ROSE AGAIN FROM THE DEAD; HE ASCENDED INTO HEAVEN AND SITTETH ON THE RIGHT HAND OF GOD THE FATHER ALMIGHTY.

VII.

FROM THENCE HE SHALL COME TO JUDGE THE QUICK AND THE DEAD.

VIII.

I BELIEVE IN THE HOLY GHOST.

IX.

THE HOLY CATHOLIC CHURCH: THE COMMUNION OF SAINTS.

X.

THE FORGIVENESS OF SINS: THE RESURRECTION OF THE BODY.

XI.

THE LIFE ETERNAL.

NOTE I.

The Idea of Religion.

NOTE II.

THE IDEA OF FAITH.

NOTE III.

THE CREEDS.

NOTE IV.

THE DIVINE FATHERHOOD.

NOTE V.

ALL-SOVEREIGN AND ALMIGHTY.

NOTE VI.

The Christology of the New Testament.

NOTE VII.

The Universality of the Character of the Lord.

(*Extracts from a Lecture by* Mr Goldwin Smith.)

NOTE VIII.

The Blood of Christ.

NOTE IX.

The Communion of Saints.

I.

FAITH.

Faith is the substance of things hoped for, the test of things not seen.

HEBR. xi. 1.

I believe; help Thou mine unbelief.

MARK ix. 24.

Great is thy faith: be it done unto thee even as thou wilt.

MATTH. xv. 28.

IN the course of the following Lectures I propose I.
to point out what appears to me to be the force of the main articles of the Apostles' Creed, the Creed of our Baptism, the one Confession of Faith which has been the immemorial bond of Western Christendom. But before we can speak of a Creed, of the object of Faith, we must speak of Faith itself, which is the life of Creeds. The Creed is the word, but Faith is the power which appropriates it.

What then is Faith? If I were to say that it is the absolute condition of all life, of all action, of all thought which goes beyond the limitations of our own minds, I should use no exaggeration. Why do I believe and *act as believing* that the sun will rise to-morrow? that the friend or the father will not fail me in my need? that wrong will not for ever go unpunished? No experience can ever penetrate the future while it is future; and the past *in itself* can give no pledge

I. for that which will be. These are truths which, as far as I can see, are wholly beyond question. Yet we do not rest in them, as if they expressed the whole truth. We ourselves add from ourselves that which gives general validity to the results of observation. We affirm, we are so constituted as to affirm when the discipline of life has done its work, that the phenomena of nature are not arbitrary, disconnected events, but the expression of one fixed will: that character is not a transient manifestation of chance feeling, but a solid growth bearing its proper fruit: that good and evil are not names alterable at man's pleasure, but signs of that which he was born to fulfil and to abhor. By Faith, that is, in dealing with the commonest circumstances of life, we penetrate the future, we enter on the unseen: we grasp it, we embody it, we try it, we commit ourselves to it with a confidence which nothing can shake. Belief deals with that which has been or with that which now is. Faith claims as its own that which is not yet brought within the range of sense. It is clear then that we cannot get quit of our dependence upon Faith by doing away with Religion. We live by Faith however we live. Perhaps, it is a sad possibility, we can die without it.

But while Faith does thus underlie all life it

finds its most characteristic exercise in spiritual I.
things. Spiritual things are in a peculiar sense unseen and eternal. Other things pass, as it were, from earth out of sight, out of time; but these come to us from that loftier, sightless, timeless order to which they properly belong. None the less they belong also to us. As we were made to live in relation to the visible, we were made to live also in relation to the invisible. We were made to seek God, made to seek the One, made to seek unity in the many parts of our own personal nature, unity in our relations to the great world in which we are placed, unity in our relations to Him in Whom we are. Religion is the striving, however imperfectly, partially, even unconsciously, after this unity; and it is by Faith that we are enabled to make the effort to gain it. In this aspect, to borrow the image of the Patriarch's dream, Faith is as the ladder joining earth and heaven on which the angels of God find footing as they fulfil their ministries of love.

But here we have great need of caution. The very breadth and grandeur and necessity of Faith cause it to be marred by many disguises and simulated by many counterfeits, such as credulity and superstition and conviction of the truth of a thing. Credulity is not Faith. That indolent abdication of the responsibility of judgment in

I. favour of every pretender, that superficial assent lightly given and lightly withdrawn, is utterly at variance with the intense clear vision and with the resolute grasp of Faith.

Superstition is not Faith. To choose for ourselves idols, whatever they may be, to invest with attributes of the unseen world fragments of this world, to brood over shadows, is to deny Faith, which is at every moment active, progressive, busy with the infinite.

Conviction is not Faith. We may yield to what we admit to be an inevitable intellectual conclusion. Our opposition may be silenced or vanquished. But the state of mind which is thus produced is very often simply a state of exhaustion and not of quickening. Till the heart welcomes the Truth, it remains outside us. As a mere logical result, we have no sympathy with it. It does not in virtue of its own nature enter into us to fill up a void in our being.

Setting aside then these and other like counterfeits, we ask again, What is Faith? What especially is religious Faith? It is an old, old question; and yet like the oldest questions it is ever new. For the word Faith, like the words God and Truth and Life, does not stand for one fixed, defined, dead idea. It sums up all the experience which men have gained of a vital power. The

parables of being on which we look change with I.
the widening of thought: so too do the interpretations of them; and it is through these interpretations that our conceptions of the greatest objects of the mind are filled up. Each generation therefore of necessity is able to apprehend something more of that which the word Faith represents. But nevertheless the essential properties of Faith always remain the same.

Faith is in every age, under all circumstances, that by which man lays hold on the realities which Hebr. xi. 1.
underlie the changeful appearances of things, and gives substance to hope, that by which he enters into actual communion with the powers of the unseen world and brings their manifestation to a sovereign test. It is the harmony of reason and feeling and purpose. It is, to say all briefly, thought illuminated by emotion and concentrated by will. By this energy the creature is lifted out of the limits of self. By this 'the person' in all his fulness reaches forth to the completion of his individuality. By this the believer strives forward to that fellowship in which alone is rest: he is in God and God in him. So Faith is consummated, and in the consummation we see written large the characters which mark in a rudimentary shape the commonest actions of our daily lives. Faith in God illuminates that faith

I. in law, in character, in right, which we have as made in the image of GOD.

When we think of these things we see what Faith is in its essence; and we ask next what is it in its application?

Faith—and I speak now of Faith in its completest form, of religious Faith—Faith, I answer, as applied to our present life is a principle of knowledge, a principle of power, a principle of action. It may be quickened and intensified: it may be dulled and neglected. As it is used so it will be fruitful; and we are severally responsible for the use which we make of it.

Faith is a principle of knowledge. Just as thought turned inwards lays open the laws of our own minds: just as thought turned outwards notes the recurrences of the visible order: so revelation tells us what we can as yet know of the invisible and eternal world, and Faith makes the message her own. We cannot obtain the facts of this higher order in any other way. If we are to have the knowledge it must be brought to us. We are so constituted that we can recognise the validity of a new revelation. We can welcome the message with assurance, but we cannot draw it out of ourselves: we cannot lift up our bodies above the earth, much less our souls. The truth is forced upon us at every turn. Reason is unable

to rise beyond the bounds of our personal powers. I.
Reason is baffled by the contrast, by the coexistence, of God and man. Reason stands paralysed at the grave.

In this sense it is most true that we believe in order that we may know: most true that Faith goes before understanding. For Faith gives us the facts on which we can build our conclusions afterwards. It is as the eye of the soul which penetrates into new regions and gathers new treasures for the exercise of thought. There cannot then be any rivalry, or opposition, between Reason and religious Faith. They move in regions which are absolutely distinct. When Faith has done her work, the work of Reason begins; and conversely the peculiar work of Faith begins at the very point where the work of Reason is ended. Faith carries the believer forward where Reason acknowledges the bar to its own advance. Faith sees the assurance of the unity of being in the gathering up of all things in the Son of God. Faith sees the reconciliation of the finite and the Infinite in the Incarnation of the Word. Faith sees the certainty of a future life in the Resurrection of Christ. Reason, it may be, accepts these facts of Faith and in their light interprets the guesses and the aspirations of mankind, resolves the discords of

I. our manifold existence into their primal harmony, traces onward the convergence of the lines of life to their common centre. It recognises in them the satisfaction of the aspirations and of the constitution of man. This is its appropriate office. But the facts themselves are gained by Faith. Faith is a principle of knowledge.

Again: Faith is a principle of power. If we were to listen to some we might suppose that Faith is the portion of childhood and old age, an infirmity of the weak and the ignorant. And yet, if we will be honest with ourselves, we shall confess that there is nothing great and noble in the world, nothing which calls forth the admiration and the love of men, which is not sealed with the sign of Faith. To feel the reality of something above us, above our temporal experience, above the limit of our single lives; of something more enduring than the shows which we see, more glorious than the visions which we frame; is just so far to rise to the possibility of a more transcending triumph. It cannot indeed but be so. For Faith not only apprehends the unseen, but enters into vital union with it, and so wields, according to its strength, the powers of the world to come. We all know what is the sustaining, inspiring, compelling force which a great name, or a great empire, or a great cause brings

with it. And GOD offers us all, whatever we may I.
seem to be, a name with which no earthly nobility can compare, a citizenship which brings a loftier dignity than the proudest inheritance of national glory, a cause of which all other causes able to move us by the claims of purity and knowledge and freedom and justice are but fragments and contributories. If we can by faith welcome the divine gift, knowledge will pass into love; and love will nerve with might. Faith is a principle of power.

Once again: Faith is a principle of action. There was a time when it was usual to draw a sharp line between religious and worldly things. That time has happily gone by. We all at last acknowledge more or less that all life is one. But perhaps our temptation now is to acquiesce in worldly motives for right-doing: to stop short of the clear confession both to ourselves and to others that as citizens and workers we take our share in public business, we labour to fulfil our appointed task, because the love of Christ constraineth us. And yet I do not see that any other motive has that permanence, that energy, that universality, which can support our efforts through failure, or make them independent of praise, or bring them into harmony with the countless activities of life.

I. If we do believe that Christ the Son of God came down from heaven to earth and drew all men to Him upon the Cross, then even in our humiliations and defeats we shall be enabled to wait and trust. If we do believe that He is with us all the days—through the days of sunshine and the days of gloom—we shall need no other voice to cheer us in sadness. If we do believe that in Him all things in earth and in heaven are by the divine will reconciled to God, then we shall be assured that there is something greater than our jealousies and rivalries and divisions. And if we do believe this, if we feel the inspiration of this knowledge, if we feel the stirring of this power within us, we shall not stand idle while the great stream of human affairs rolls by us. Our indifference would be our condemnation. Faith—our Christian Faith—is a principle of action.

Faith, I repeat, is in its essence the power by which we grasp the future, the unseen, the infinite, the eternal; and in its application it is a principle of knowledge, a principle of power, a principle of action. It is then on man's side the condition and the measure of divine blessing. By faith we lift up the sightless eye and it is opened: by faith we stretch out the withered arm and it is made whole: by faith, bound hand and foot with grave-cloths, we come forth from the tomb of custom which lies upon us I.

> with a weight
> Heavy as frost and deep almost as life.

For ourselves then, what is Faith to us, this sovereign power which can see, use, dwell in the heaven which lies about us still? Our answer to that question is the revelation of our life. It cannot be lightly made, and it cannot be wisely refused. It will shew us what we aim at doing, and what we can do. It will find expression not in word but in deed.

What is Faith to us? Perhaps as we come to feel more distinctly what it is capable of being, we shall answer best, mindful of our selfishness, of our triviality, of our forgetfulness of God, by praying that whatever it is it may hereafter be far more.

For a time, or even to the last, Faith will be chequered, not with doubt indeed but with darkness, when we look upon the great sorrows of life and the vain efforts of good men to remove them; but the faith which confesses its imperfection is not unrewarded.

If only we can repeat the Apostles' petition when our work is marred by the fault of others: *Lord, increase our faith—*

I. If only we can make our own that utterance of love which struggled against the bitterness of disappointment: *Lord, I believe, help Thou mine unbelief*—

If only we can bear the trial of delay and accept the judgment which lays bare our true condition—we shall in due time hear in our souls the voice which reveals blessings through trial and crowns endurance with the fulness of joy:

Great is thy faith; be it unto thee even as thou wilt.

II.

CREEDS.

Ye became obedient from the heart to that form of teaching whereunto ye were delivered.

ROM. vi. 17.

Hold the pattern of sound words which thou hast heard from me.

2 TIM. i. 13.

Let us hold fast the confession of our hope that it waver not.

HEBR. x. 23.

WE have seen that every life is guided II.
by Faith of some kind so far as it is of necessity directed by and to the future and the unseen. And Faith implies a Creed. The Creed may be earthly, mean, debasing; but no man can be without a Creed by which he shapes his conduct. This one, for example, has Faith in the power of money or authority or honour to bring happiness; and he strains every nerve to secure that which he has not tested by experience. That one has Faith in the calm of personal concentration, in self-culture, in withdrawal from the rude turmoils of society; and he closes his eyes and his heart against the sins and sorrows of the multitude. A third has Faith in knowledge or material improvement; and he throws all his energy into the bettering of the present conditions of life. Such men do not say in words 'I believe in riches' or 'in influence,' or 'in self-indulgence,' or 'in secularism,' but they

II. say so in action; and they do not hold their faith in vain. For in these and in countless other forms we can see how a real Creed is able to mould and to arm a whole nature. Faith in wealth or in strong battalions or in refined ease or in social progress produces great results before our eyes every day. Even this kind of faith does in some sense preoccupy the unseen and realise the future.

Thus the man of business and the man of pleasure has a Creed which is the strength of his life. The Christian also has his proper Creed. His Faith has an object wider, deeper, vaster, more enduring than the objects of form and sense, of which all that *is* is but a shadow and a sign. He believes not in a principle or a thought but in a Person; not in himself or in mankind, but in the Lord Jesus Christ. How this Faith must be progressively effective we shall, I hope, see as we come to consider the different facts which it embraces, but at present I wish to suggest some reflections of a more general kind, and to shew why it is both necessary and helpful that the object of our Christian Faith should find expression in a form of words; and how the Apostles' Creed, our sacred heritage only less old than the New Testament, is in its outline as broad as life.

A form of words embodies, so to speak, the unseen object of our Faith. The citizen of the world is not called upon to put his creed into set language. In many cases he would shrink from doing so; and under any circumstances that which he prizes—wealth, rule, glory—is open to all eyes. There is no need to recall such things to the thoughts of those who have their faith in them. But with spiritual objects it is otherwise. Here we require to remind ourselves and to remind one another of the Invisible in which we trust: to bring this which we cannot handle or measure within the range of constant experience: to claim for it a place among the recognised powers of life. II.

So we find, handed down to us as a priceless inheritance, words to define our Faith; and then we openly proclaim it. Such confession gives a positive distinctness to aspiration. Such confession offers a watchword for effort and a guide to devotion. And again this confession of our Faith in a form of words answers to a natural impulse of the soul. The first work of the man who has grasped the unseen will be to make known the blessing which he has found. He who believes in GOD, in the Father and the Son and the Holy Spirit, will be constrained to express his belief. The truth

II. on which he has laid hold concerns others and not himself only. It is a treasure which grows greater by impartment. For while our Christian Faith is personal it is social also. While we each say '*I* believe' with the fulness of individual conviction and not simply '*we* believe,' we say it in conscious fellowship with those about us. And this separate confession, if we reflect upon it, makes our union more real and more close.

In this way a formal Creed witnesses to the universality of our Faith. I join with others in repeating it that I may declare openly that the facts which meet my wants, which satisfy my instincts, are for all men. My apprehension of them is not the measure of their efficacy or of their meaning. Nay rather, as I find in them what I require, my heart is enlarged to sympathise with those who find in them the answer to other needs. In this way a common Creed enables me to learn more of myself as well as more of the Gospel.

Constant habit deadens our sense of the grandeur of this communion of faith. Yet the great truth remains ready for our use. If only a single congregation could enter into full possession of all that lies in this acknowledgment of the divine allegiance which we agree to profess: if we could each feel, and then all act together as feeling,

that faith in God as He has revealed Himself II.
is the foundation, the rule, the life of our lives: there would be a force present to move the world. And then let us extend our thoughts, and remember that the confession which we make is made practically in the same form from day to day by countless congregations in Western Christendom, and we shall know that that which we have in common with all who bear Christ's name, is greater, immeasurably greater, than the special beliefs, however precious to ourselves, however perverse and wilful and unfounded in the eyes of others, which keep, and which must keep us apart.

Nor may we stop here. The Creed which thus binds us all together now, even in spite of ourselves, binds us to all the past. The history of the Church is indeed sadly chequered, but there is no other history which can be compared with it; and from the first the Apostles' Creed was substantially the symbol of its heroes. Interpretations, glosses, enlargements were added, but the outline at least was fixed in the second century, fixed unchangeably. And I cannot suppose that any one is insensible to the influence of this testimony of ages. As often as we repeat the Creed of our Baptism we repeat the words by which martyrs have lived and died, the

II. words under which new nations have been enrolled as soldiers in Christ's army, the words which have remained through every vicissitude the standard of the Christian belief. And he must be something less than man who is not moved by the power of this unbroken fellowship with the past, which makes us heirs of every victory of Faith.

Another thought flows directly from this. The Creed which unites us with all the past, preserves for us the complete and harmonious outline of the foundations of Faith. As time goes on, now this part of it, now that comes into prominence. It is only by a serious effort that we can recognise the due proportion which the parts bear to one another as we regard them from our own point of view. But the Creed is of no one age. As often as we repeat it we are guarded from forgetting the articles which our circumstances do not force upon our notice. All the facts remain, and when a crisis comes that will be ready to our hand which our fathers have delivered to us. We want nothing new, but the old rekindled by a fuller light.

To these manifold services of a Creed one more may be added. Such a summary as the Apostles' Creed serves as a clue in reading the Bible. It presents to us the salient features in the revelation which earlier experience has proved to be

turning-points of spiritual knowledge. It offers II.
centres, so to speak, round which we may group our thoughts, and to which we may refer the lessons laid open to us. It keeps us from wandering in by-paths aimlessly or at our will, not by fixing arbitrary limits to inquiry but by marking the great lines along which believers have moved from the first.

To a certain extent any Creed sanctioned by the use of many centuries would have these advantages; but if we look a little more closely at the Apostles' Creed, which has been in our minds all along, we shall see that it is fitted to bring them all to us in richest abundance. It is the spontaneous expression of the life, of the feeling, of the experience, of the Christian Society. Though it is not an Apostles' Creed in that literal sense with which mediæval art has familiarised us; though we may not suppose that each apostle contributed one clause to make up the harmonious sum; it is the Apostles' Creed in a deeper sense as embodying the first Gospel in its original form, the Gospel of St Peter and St Paul, of St Andrew, St Bartholomew and St Thomas, which we see shadowed forth in their own confessions. Thus the Apostles' Creed is truly apostolic, and, which more directly perhaps concerns us, it is personal and it is historical.

II. It is personal. We have seen that it is personal on our part: that it is the distinct voice of the belief of each one of us (*I believe*); but far more than this: it is personal in its object. It expresses not the conviction that something is true, but that some One is the stay of life. We do not say 'I believe that there is a God,' that 'Jesus Christ came to earth,' that 'the Holy Ghost was sent to men.' In this sense, as St James says, 'the devils believe and tremble.' But we say 'I believe in God the Father,' 'I believe in Jesus Christ,' 'I believe in the Holy Ghost.' That is, I do not simply acknowledge the existence of these Divine Persons of the one Godhead but I throw myself wholly upon their power and love. I have found and I trust without reserve Him Who made, redeemed, sanctifies me. I have gained not a certain conclusion but an unfailing, an all-powerful, Friend. 'I believe in Him.' He can help me; and He will help me.

We feel at once when the thought is set before us how this characteristic of our Creed brings it *into* our life. It is the expression of personal trust and not simply of intellectual conviction. The most unquestioned and unquestionable propositions lie outside us. We take account of them: we regulate our conduct by them: they may move us with hope or even with enthusiasm; but they

leave us alone. Faith in God, on the other hand, II.
witnesses to a fellowship able to penetrate and hallow our whole being, active in us at every moment, bringing to us the powers of another world.

In this most momentous sense our Creed is personal. It is also, as I said, historical. We believe in God, and we declare His nature by recounting what He has done in the limits of time and space. We do not attempt to describe His essence or His attributes in abstract language. We speak of His works and through these we form in our human ways some conception of what He is.

Thus we confess that we *believe*

In God the Father Almighty, Maker of heaven and earth:

In Jesus Christ His only Son Who was born, Who died, rose again, ascended, and shall come again:

In the Holy Ghost; and, as the manifestation of His unseen action, *we believe,* not in the Holy Catholic Church, but, *that there is a Holy Catholic Church, a Communion of Saints, Forgiveness of Sins, Resurrection of the Body and Life everlasting.*

No interpretation of these great facts is added. They belong to life. They are in themselves

II. unchangeable. They stand before us for ever in their sublime majesty, part of the history of the world. They are unchangeable; but as the years teach us more of the conditions of our own present existence, we see more of the divine revelation which they convey. So we interpret them for ourselves. But we shall be slow to place our conclusions, even the simplest, by the side of the primary facts. Where the wilfulness of false teaching has made such addition necessary, as in the Nicene Creed, the addition is, under some aspects, a loss. It is at the best a safeguard against error, and not, as we are tempted to think, an increase of spiritual knowledge. Our knowledge of GOD must be man's knowledge, and therefore not a knowledge of Him as He is, dwelling in light unapproachable, but a knowledge of His relations to ourselves so far as He has made them known. It is this knowledge, the knowledge of GOD'S work on earth, the spring and the assurance of access, of fellowship, of devotion, and not the knowledge of the schools, the technical arrangement of formal conclusions, which the Apostles' Creed brings before us. It is this knowledge coming through life which touches life. It is this knowledge which enables us to listen to the voice of the divine Commandments and offer our prayer to our Father in heaven. It is this knowledge to which 'we have been delivered' that it may mould and keep us, body, soul, and spirit, until the day of the Lord. II.

'To which we have been delivered.' It is a most startling phrase; yet this is literally what St Paul says when he speaks of the Christian Creed. He does not write: '*ye obeyed from the heart that form of doctrine which was delivered you,*'—that is but a small part of the truth,—but '*that form of doctrine whereunto ye were delivered.*' The phrase is as startling as it is openly true. Our Creed, whatever it really is, is our sovereign master, or rather our inspiring power. It calls out our energies. It directs their application. It exacts our service. We can have no escape from its dominion: no rest from its influence. 'We are delivered to it:' perhaps as the unconscious victims of a degrading thraldom, perhaps as the eager servants of that which we have gladly recognised to be a divine will.

Feeling then what a Creed is, what our Creed is, we approach the study of its contents with surer confidence, in order that we may learn better that it is able to guard, to support, to animate us: that it has strength to fashion our lives in health and sickness, in joy and sorrow, in

II. thought and action, after a godlike type: strength to correct us with the authority of an inviolable law: strength to fill us with the enthusiasm of a living faith.

III.

I BELIEVE IN GOD THE FATHER, ALMIGHTY, MAKER OF HEAVEN AND EARTH.

God that made the world and all things therein...made of one every nation of men...that they should seek God, if haply they might feel after Him and find Him, though He is not far from each one of us; for in Him we live and move and have our being.

ACTS xvii. 24—28.

To us there is one God, the Father, of Whom are all things, and we unto Him.

1 COR. viii. 6.

God is spirit.

JOHN iv. 24.

God is light.

1 JOHN i. 5.

God is love.

1 JOHN iv. 8, 16.

Our God is a consuming fire.

DEUT. iv. 24; HEBR. xii. 29.

WE have spoken of Faith which is the power of life, and of the Creed which sets before us the object of our Christian Faith. The Apostles' Creed is, as we have seen, personal and historical. It offers to us a GOD on Whom we can throw ourselves for guidance and support, and not a series of abstract propositions which we must hold as true. It enables us to form a conception of His nature from the record of what He has done, as Creator, Redeemer, Sanctifier, a conception which as it is brought to us through life gains in fulness and clearness as our knowledge of life is enlarged either by our individual experience, or by the accumulated experience of mankind. III.

The Apostles' Creed, I repeat, shews GOD to us, the One GOD, as our Creator, Redeemer, Sanctifier, and we acknowledge under each relation what He has done, is doing and will do for us, that so we may gain strength and wisdom for

III. the accomplishment of our own duty to Him, to our neighbour and to ourselves. Each of the main aspects of this threefold divine work will come under notice in due order. We have now to consider the first article in which our Faith finds expression for its confidence: *I believe in God, the Father, Almighty, Maker of heaven and earth,* words which bear witness to the highest power and the true end of man; words which include all that is made plainer to us by the slow unfolding of the divine purpose; words which fix for ever our fellowship with God, our fellowship one with another, our fellowship, I will venture to say, with all the works of God.

I believe in God. To say this is to confess that there is something greater than our minds, greater than our hearts, to which we can aspire with love answering to love: something which thought can touch, so to speak, but neither prove nor measure, which affection can reach after and yet not everywhere embrace.

I believe in God. To say this is to confess that there is, in spite of every unpunished sin, every fruitless sorrow (as we judge), one purpose of victorious righteousness being fulfilled about us and in us, one purpose able to reconcile justice and mercy in the complete accomplishment of the destiny of creation.

I believe in God. To say this is to confess that we are not alone, ourselves, our families, our nation, our race, and yet that we are alone: not alone because we are bound to countless forms of finite being visible and invisible, alone, individually alone, because the full harmony of the universe depends upon the presence in due measure of all the parts, even of that feeblest part, which is inaudible it may be to our ears. III.

I believe in God. To say this is to confess that we stand each as children face to face with Him Whom the heaven of heavens cannot contain: to confess that the preservation of the world depends on Him Who made it: to confess that there is a unity of being of which there is one source and one end, that there is, in the words of St Paul, *one God, the Father, of Whom are all things and we unto Him.*

These are the thoughts which we have to seek to bring into our life, thoughts of the unsearchable Majesty, and the unfailing Providence of God, of the endless variety and supreme unity of His creation, thoughts which at once pass into prayers. Someone has spoken of 'the knees of the soul.' So may we bend now on 'the knees of our souls,' as we meditate very shortly on each clause in the first Article of our Faith.

I believe in God. The declaration of our

dependence is in harmony with all that our reason can establish, but it does not depend upon our reason. No argument which we can draw either from the consideration of ourselves or from the consideration of the world can carry us to the conclusion in which alone we find strength and rest. The GOD Whom the soul sees dimly and to Whom it turns as the flower turns to the sun is greater than His works shew Him, greater than our minds can measure. It is true that every argument from design and from conscience, from being which underlies phenomena and from being which underlies thought, suggests to us, as we are able to follow the indications, something more as to the nature and working of Him after Whom our whole manhood feels and in Whom it can repose; but such arguments illuminate the conception and do not create it or prove its truth. The idea of GOD, the idea of One who is described most completely as 'Spirit,' 'Light,' 'Love,' 'Fire,' of absolute righteousness and power and mercy, answers to the maturity of man's growth, as light answers to the eye. We were made to recognise Him, and He has made Himself known.

So we go on a step further. *I believe,* we say, *in GOD, the Father.* In this connexion the title Father is a gift of the Gospel. The oldest Greek poets spoke of Zeus as 'the father of gods and men' under the imagery of patriarchal life, and they made Him like to themselves. Philosophers spoke of the Father of the universe, recognising something more than an arbitrary connexion between the Creator and the Creation, but they added that "it is hard to gain a knowledge of Him and impossible to communicate it to the world." The Hebrew Prophets spoke of the Lord as the Father of Israel, forming and disciplining the chosen people with a wise and tender love. But Christ first added the title 'my Father' to that of 'our Father.' It is through the revelation of the Son that we can find each our personal fellowship with a Father in heaven. And at the same time it is through the revelation of the Son that the idea of Fatherhood is shewn to lie in the very Nature of the Godhead itself. In the Life and Death of Christ there is a revelation unexhausted and inexhaustible of the Father, His Father and our Father. The answer to the prayer '*Shew us the Father,*' which is ever rising in some form or other to the disciple's lips, will be to the end of time: '*Have I*—I, the Son of Man, the Son of GOD—*been so long time with you and dost thou not know Me?*' hast thou not yet read the lesson III.

III. of a life laid down that it might be taken up again, of death conquered, of heaven entered and laid open? hast thou not found in this manifestation of GOD's will and love and power, Him in Whom faith gains a distinct object, and affection the fulness of a devout service?

Thus our personal want is satisfied. We see 'the Father' in the record of Christ's personal life wrought out under the conditions of human effort and suffering. But we are men and among men. We are citizens. We are children and parents. We share a life wider than our own. Looking to these facts, full of solemn and unutterable mysteries, we say, *I believe in GOD, the Father, Almighty,* or rather if we may endeavour to express the force of the original term, *All-sovereign.* For the title is not descriptive of abstract power but of exercised dominion. It is used in the Greek version of the Old Testament to represent what stands in our English Bible as 'the Lord of hosts,' the King Who sways by His will the course of all finite being. When then we say, *I believe in GOD, the Father, Almighty,* we confess that the Father to Whom the heart of His children can turn in trustful confidence is the Ruler of the world, the Ruler of the worlds. This is a faith which it is alike difficult to grasp and impossible to surrender. We cannot give up the belief that there is a purpose and an order and an end in what often seem the blind tumults of nations. We cannot give it up, and yet 'here and here' perhaps we cannot justify it. We may rejoice then that the one Creed of our Baptism lifts up our thoughts to a higher level: that it extends the scene on which the issues of life are played out: that it places all that we see in connexion with the eternal. Scripture indeed does not veil the darknesses of life while it reveals the light. It speaks most significantly of powers of evil as 'world-sovereign,' but none the less it proclaims without one note of hesitancy that God is 'All-sovereign.' The end is not here, and it is not yet. Meanwhile we can hold our faith and say in spite of tyrannies which crush for ages the powers of nations, of ambitions which squander them with prodigal selfishness, of passions which divide and neutralise them: 'I look further than my present sight reaches. 'I carry forward my hope to an order where this 'order will find its consummation. I appeal to 'the tribunal of a sovereign Judge, whose will 'is right and whose will must prevail: *I believe 'in God the Father, Almighty.*' III.

The earliest Western Creed added no more. This was the whole of the first article. It

III seemed enough to acknowledge God's dealings with the individual soul and with the world, as Father and Ruler. But at a later time a clause was borrowed from the East which completes our confession and we were taught to say: *I believe in God the Father, Almighty, Maker of heaven and earth.*

The addition was not without a weighty purpose. This acknowledgment of God as the Creator of things visible and invisible brings with it many deep and helpful thoughts. It reminds us that as all that is came into existence by the will and power of God, so it is sustained by Him alone; for the fact of creation involves the necessity of preservation, of unfolding. It reminds us that the greatest and least objects by which we are surrounded, the Sun in its glory and the stars in their countless multitude: *mountains and all hills: fruitful trees and all cedars: beasts and all cattle: worms and feathered fowls* were made by Him who made us, and that they therefore fill a place in His vast counsel of love, and minister to His glory. It reminds us of the truth, which others are beginning to tell us with stern reproaches, that we cannot separate ourselves from the material world of which we are a part; but in doing so it does not mockingly thrust man down to the level of the earth, but

it offers to him the hope that the earth shall share III.
the glory of his redemption.

So the first article of our Creed reaches its amplest range. We confess that the God who is the soul's necessity has been revealed to us in Christ as the Father, is indicated by history as All-sovereign, is declared by nature as Maker of heaven and earth. Reaching out to these realities of life, pondering our connexion with the world, with humanity, with God, striving to give fuller distinctness to that which we apprehend vaguely, labouring now and again to bring the little details and difficulties of duty into the light of our confession, we say one to another I and I and I *believe in God the Father, Almighty, Maker of heaven and earth.*

We say so and Christ's words sound in our ears, *Do ye now believe?* It is indeed the question of all questions. For, as I said before, our belief in God is not a matter of speculation or of customary form, of light controversy or hasty speech. The name, the thought of God may well fill us with wordless awe. He of Whom we Eccles. v. 1, 2.
speak is so near and yet so infinitely unapproachable, so 'questionable' and yet so past finding out, that every confession seems to claim as its sequel a space of silent adoration. It is otherwise with the fashionable idols of man's

III. making. But for us GOD cannot be simply the august symbol of the authority with which we invest a varying collection of principles and laws: the ideal centre to which we can bring together the choice offerings of culture and art: the postulate or the necessary conclusion of human reason, which requires that which is eternal beneath the shows of time. Not so: taught by our Creed we look to One Who rules with that freedom which is perfect justice: for One Whom we can serve with the devotion of our whole nature and Who welcomes our service: for One Who quickens, guides, inspires the individual soul with the influence of a real fellowship, love calling out and answering love, *He in us* that we may be enabled to fulfil our part in the conflicts of a chequered life, *we in Him* that we may rise in faith to the calmness of that 'rest of GOD' which is work without toil.

Do ye now believe? It is a question which concerns the present even more than the past. It is not enough to hold that GOD did great things for our fathers: not enough to pride ourselves on the inheritance of victories of faith: not enough to build the sepulchres of those who were martyred by men unwilling in their day of trial as we may be in our own to hear new voices of a living GOD. Our duty is to see whether GOD is

with us. Whether we expect great things from I.
Him. Whether we do not practically place Him far off, forgetting that if He *is*, He is about us, speaking to us words which have not been heard before, guiding us to paths on which earlier generations have not been able to enter. There is, most terrible thought, a practical atheism, orthodox in language and reverent in bearing, which can enter a Christian Church and charm the conscience to rest with shadowy traditions, an atheism which grows insensibly within us if we separate what cannot be separated with impunity, the secular from the divine, the past and the future from the present, earth from heaven, the things of Caesar from the things of God.

Do ye now believe? We read of the conflicts of nations and take account of what seem to be the motives, selfish and unworthy, of those who direct them : we go into the highways of our cities and measure in the idle loungers the waste of energy, physical, moral, spiritual, enough to arm a new and nobler Crusade : we look into our own hearts and see with something of startled surprise how small a place is occupied by the thought of God, while we are confident in the strength which He has lent, and sanguine with the hope which He has inspired : and we pause perhaps before we make reply.

III. If we do pause let us thank God that He has again called us to Himself. By that arrested thought He makes known that He is waiting to teach us: waiting to teach us in silence of our heart's watches, in the distractions of our business, through the temptations which lead us to self-indulgence and self-assertion, which persuade us to appeal to low impulses and to seek easy successes, which embolden us to put aside fresh truths because they will not conveniently fit into the scheme of the world which we have made. Even so let us now thank God, Who is waiting to teach us that we may confess more intelligently and more actively the source from which we came and the end for which we were made; waiting to teach us that our lives may witness by the power of their influence and the singleness of their aim that for us there is *one God, the Father, of Whom are all things and we unto Him.*

IV.

AND IN JESUS CHRIST HIS ONLY SON OUR LORD.

To us...there is one Lord, Jesus Christ, through whom are all things and we through Him.

1 Cor. viii. 6.

In the beginning was the Word, and the Word was with GOD, *and the Word was* GOD*...and the Word became flesh.*

John i. 1, 14.

Philip saith unto Him: Lord, shew us the Father, and it sufficeth us. Jesus saith unto him, Have I been so long time with you, and dost thou not know Me, Philip? he that hath seen Me hath seen the Father.

John xiv. 8, 9.

I ascend to My Father and your Father, and My GOD *and your* GOD.

John xx. 17.

We have not a High Priest that cannot be touched with the feeling of our infirmities; but one that hath been in all points tempted like as we are, yet without sin.

Hebr. iv. 15.

WHEN we attempt to follow out the main thoughts suggested by the Creed as to our belief in GOD, the Father, All-sovereign, Creator of heaven and earth, it cannot but be that we find ourselves in danger of being lost in unsearchable mysteries. Every effort to give distinctness to the idea of GOD in Himself ends by limiting that which is unlimited. The action of Providence is so complicated and on so vast a scale that in our endeavours to follow it we commonly do no more than isolate a few events from the broad stream of which they are a part. The workings of physical law are so stern and inexorable that hope and love lose the freshness of their energy under the hard discipline of experience. As we learn more of the weakness of our own powers, more of the vastness of history, more of the unvarying forces of nature, GOD the All-sovereign the Creator seems to be withdrawn further and further from us. The præ-Christian history of the world is the record of this sorrowful truth. IV.

IV. And as we realise it, each one in our own life, as we must do, we find ourselves, half-unconsciously, repeating the prayer which summed up the desire
John xiv. 8. of the old world: *Lord, shew us the Father, and it sufficeth us:* give us, that is, a vision of GOD in some shape which we can understand, which belongs to actual life, which will grow with our growth, and we ask, we need no more.

Now as then the answer to this prayer has been already given, the sight has been already granted, though word and revelation be dimly understood or altogether unregarded. The Lord
John xiv. 1. has said before we speak: *Let not your heart be troubled, neither let it be afraid. Believe in GOD: believe also in Me.*

Following, striving to follow, this command we say in the Apostles' Creed not only *I believe in GOD the Father, Almighty, Maker of heaven and earth*, but also *I believe in Jesus Christ, His only Son, our Lord.* What then do we mean by our confession? This is the question which we must try to answer now.

As we consider the words we shall see that they contain two main statements which set before us the Person and the Nature of Him in Whom we are taught to see the Father.

I believe in Jesus Christ. Here is the Person in Whom we trust.

I believe in Him as *the only Son* of GOD, *our Lord.* Here is the description of His Nature in regard to GOD and to ourselves. IV.

I believe in Jesus Christ. These simple words are a Creed in themselves. The phrase *Jesus Christ* is more than a name, more than a title. It expresses that One truly man fulfilled a divine office, that Jesus Who was born, suffered, died on earth, is the Christ, the hope of Israel, the hope of the world. And we declare our belief in Him as true man and as the Christ.

The thought of Jesus the Saviour—shadowed forth in the first who bore the name, Joshua the Conqueror of Canaan—as man, true man, perfect man, representative man, will come before us afterwards when we notice what the Creed tells us of the details of His life. Now we have to consider what we learn by acknowledging Him as the Christ, the Messiah, the Anointed.

As often as we repeat the words *I believe in Jesus Christ* we bear witness to the work of Judaism: we acknowledge how through long ages GOD was preparing a people as ministers of His will, by the vicissitudes of bondage and victory, of dominion and exile, by isolation and dispersion, by the hard restraints of the Law and by the spiritual enthusiasm of the Prophets: how the hope, which was the foundation of the race, that in them *all*

IV. *the nations of the earth should be blessed*, gained
Gen. xviii. 18; xii. 3. definiteness and power from the changeful for-
Gal. iii. 16. tunes of nearly two thousand years: how priest and king and seer and sufferer each added some new trait to the portraiture of a perfect Saviour: how at last in the fulness of time, when all things
Gal. iv. 4. were ready, One came *born of a woman*, who by the manifestation of the Truth fulfilled the office of the prophets, by the sacrifice of Himself crowned the ministry of priests and illuminated the picture of the righteous in affliction, by laying open the springs of human sympathy established on the Cross the power of an eternal kingdom.

We believe therefore in Jesus, the Christ, as the apostles proclaimed Him; but Israel did not believe. Here lies another lesson in our Creed. GOD fulfilled His promises, but He did not fulfil them as men had expected. The Lord wrought
Matt. xi. 2. *the works of the Christ* and required those who
John x. 24. witnessed them to decide who He was. He left the minds of the wilful and self-seeking in sus-
Matt. xvi. 17. pense: He welcomed the confession of faith as a direct revelation from His Father. And so it is still. Our belief in Jesus as the Christ does not come from any direct proof which relieves us of responsibility. We see in the Gospels the record of His words and deeds: we feel in our hearts the needs of life: the Spirit, by GOD's gift

connects the facts of history with the facts of conscience, and we acknowledge each for ourselves that Jesus of Nazareth is the Saviour for Whom we look, Who has brought GOD to dwell with us and in us. IV.

Thus from the Person of the Lord we go on to consider His Nature. We confess that He is 'the only Son of GOD' and 'our Lord.' In both respects, though truly man Who lived with men, He occupies a position essentially distinct from that of any other. His Godhead is one with the Godhead of the Father, His sovereignty over men is absolute. Christians are sons of GOD, but sons by adoption in virtue of their fellowship with Him Who is Son by nature. There are many lords who claim the obedience of outward service but One only Who demands the complete surrender of the soul.

We believe—I say—and confess that Jesus Christ is the only Son of GOD. The confession cannot be lightly made. If the simple thought of GOD ought to fill us with speechless awe, the further thought of GOD as Father, Son, and Holy Spirit, one GOD, is yet more overwhelming. On such a mystery, where human words and human thoughts must fail, our words should be few, and these spoken rather in devotion than in explanation or argument. Happy are we if we can yet

IV. rest in the simple language of our Baptismal Creed. We need go no further for perfect adoration and perfect confidence. It is enough for us to know that He Who lived our life, on Whom we place our trust, is the only Son of God, and therefore Himself in essence very God: to know that the realities of Fatherhood and Sonship lie in the Godhead, so that we cannot now think of the one God except as Father nor as Father without the Son: to know that *the Word*, the Logos, in the phrases of St John, He Who *was in the beginning with God*, when time began, Who was therefore with God beyond time, He *through Whom all things were made, became flesh:* to know that He Who in His human nature *can be touched with the feeling of our infirmities* is able in His divine nature *to help to the uttermost those who come to Him.*

Such knowledge is indeed most practical. If, as we have seen, the confession of God as the Creator of heaven and earth brings all things very near to us, much more does this confession of our belief in Jesus Christ the only Son of God *through Whom are all things, and we through Him.* By this confession we learn to see how that connexion of the Son with man which was completed by the Incarnation was prepared by manifold revelations of His power and love

from "the beginning;" how He was ever coming IV.
into the world which He had made, as its true 1 John i. 1.
light; how He was ever present in the world, John i. 9.
as its true life. By this confession we learn to see how He Who has redeemed us by taking our nature to Himself is the Author of every noble thought which has been uttered by unconscious prophets, of every fruitful deed of sacrifice which has been wrought by statesmen and heroes, of every triumph of insight and expression by which students and artists have interpreted the harmonies and depths of nature. So we claim for Christ with patient confidence, in spite of every misrepresentation and misunderstanding,
'whatsoever is true, and noble, and just, and pure, Phil. iv. 8.
and lovely and gracious,' whatsoever witnesses to man's proper being and rightly demands his praise; we claim all for Him *through Whom are all things,* all things which are, all things which abide in the presence of God.

In virtue of this our faith we affirm the reality of a dominion of Christ which is often unacknowledged and often denied: we welcome as fellow-subjects and fellow-labourers those who repudiate our greeting. But we do not stay here. We ourselves accept without reserve in our own case, openly and with all its consequences, the allegiance which is due to His divine sovereignty.

IV. *We believe in Jesus Christ, the only Son of GOD, our Lord:* 'our Lord,' and not vaguely 'the Lord.' The words describe plainly the position in which we stand and proclaim that we stand towards Him. Others whom He has endowed not less richly, through whom He works not less effectively, to whom He has made some parts of His will clearer than to us, may refuse to recognise His gifts, His inspiration, His teaching, but we have known Him, and take upon ourselves the obligations of His service. His will is the law of our action. His strength is the support of our efforts. His praise is the measure of our success.

But do we not in this respect—the inquiry must rise within us—expose ourselves to just reproach? Is it not true that being Christians we dissemble our motives and our hopes till we practically lose sight of them? that we hide from others first and then from ourselves the impulses by which we are most powerfully stirred, the aspirations which we most devoutly cherish? that we make the world the poorer by refusing to give it the example of what Christ has wrought in us?

Such dissimulation is beyond question better than the hypocrisy which affects lofty principles without inwardly feeling them. But it sets aside the charge which is laid upon us by our Creed to

do all things for GOD'S glory. For in apostolic IV.
language, each Christian is in due measure him- 1 John ii. 20.
self a Christ, empowered by the gift of the Holy Spirit to announce the truth which he has learnt, to apply the atonement which he has received, to establish the kingdom which he believes to be universal. Here it is, I repeat, that we fail most grievously. However repulsive the ostentation of religion may be, the suppression of faith is more perilous. Who can believe that the heart is full when the lips are silent? And in this our practice condemns us. We inherit and we use the powers of the Faith, and yet we do not make it visible that we differ from those who do not willingly accept such an inheritance. We do not follow out our belief to its issues, asking ourselves again and again what it enables us to do and to bear and to hope more than other men: asking ourselves silently till the answer comes: and then letting the answer be seen in a life which is manifestly swayed by a present consciousness of the unseen and the eternal; which rests upon the conviction that the end of our being has been made attainable by the Cross; which yields loyal obedience to a Lord the symbol of Whose sovereignty is sacrifice.

It is a truism to say that Christianity is a belief in Christ; but is it not a forgotten truism?

IV. We honour with ungrudging admiration those who labour with zeal and patience to shield the weak from injury, the poor from want, and the ignorant from temptation; who hope to elevate the condition of our artizans by giving their opinion the responsibility of power, and to discipline the improvident by ideas of comfort and self-respect: those who investigate the problems of religious thought, and seek to shew how circumstances of time and place call out this and that want, this and that belief, and lay open the manifold elements of truth which give whatever stability and strength they have to the religions of the world: those who in lonely meditation strive to reconnect man's spirit with its source. Such are *not far from the kingdom of* GOD; but as yet they are not Christians.

Christianity is not philanthropy, or philosophy, or mysticism. It realises, guides, chastens each noblest energy of man, but it is not identified with any one of them. It gives permanence and power, it gives light and support, to the many activities of body, soul, and spirit, but no one of these richest activities can take its place.

As Christians we believe in GOD: we believe also in Jesus Christ. It is, let us boldly avow it, an amazing faith. We cast the burden of our lives upon Him Who, very man, has borne it upon earth, upon Him Who has fulfilled by living, dying, rising again, every promise to Jew or Greek through which the Father encouraged the world to look for redemption and consummation: upon Him Whom we confess in the fulness of His Deity as *the only Son of God,* and in the absoluteness of His sovereignty as *our Lord.* IV.

We believe in Jesus Christ our Lord. We recognise with the deepest thankfulness the debt of reverence which we owe to all Princes and Governors, to all ministers and magistrates, to all teachers and spiritual fathers, through whom God is pleased to reveal His authority on earth. But in each of these we see only a faint and partial reflection of that supreme glory which is the source of their dignity and the ground of their existence. For us there is—and the confession is able to give its true majesty, its proper joy, its lofty meaning to every office of our daily duties—*one Lord, Jesus Christ, through Whom are all things and we through Him.*

V.

WHO WAS CONCEIVED BY THE HOLY GHOST, BORN OF THE VIRGIN MARY, SUFFERED UNDER PONTIUS PILATE, WAS CRUCIFIED, DEAD AND BURIED.

Since then the children are sharers in flesh and blood, He also Himself in like manner partook of the same; that through death He might bring to nought him that had the power of death, that is, the devil.

HEB. ii. 14.

But when the fulness of the time came, GOD *sent forth His Son, born of a woman, born under the law.*

GAL. iv. 4.

And the Word became flesh, and dwelt among us (and we beheld His glory, glory as of the only-begotten from the Father), full of grace and truth.

JOHN i. 14.

[*He*] *emptied Himself, taking the form of a servant, being made in the likeness of men; and being found in fashion as a man, He humbled Himself, becoming obedient even unto death, yea, the death of the cross.*

PHIL. ii. 7, 8.

We behold Him Who hath been made a little lower than the angels, even Jesus, because of the suffering of death crowned with glory and honour, that by the grace of GOD *He should taste death for every one.*

HEB. ii. 9.

THE summary confession of our faith in Jesus v. Christ, whereby we acknowledge Him to be the fulfiller of all the divine promises to mankind, the only Son of GOD, our Lord, is followed in the Creeds by a more particular record of His work. This falls into two parts. The first describes the work of His earthly Life: the second His work in the world of spirits, crowned by that coming to Judgment which is the union of the two.

In this lecture I propose to speak of that which the Creed teaches as to Christ's work on earth, reserving for the next the consideration of its issues in the world beyond the grave. The two subjects are indeed inseparable: they are opposite sides of the same realities. Yet to our apprehension they appear as cause and effect. *Jesus Christ*, St Paul writes, *became* Phil. ii. 8f. *obedient unto death even the death of the Cross; wherefore also GOD highly exalted Him.* And again it is written, *we see Him Who hath been* Hebr. ii. 9. *made a little lower than the angels, even Jesus, because of the suffering of death, crowned with*

v. *glory and honour.* So He in His humanity
—Jesus—accomplished the true destiny of man, and accomplished through suffering the destiny of man fallen.

We do well therefore to consider by itself Christ's earthly life, to use whatever helps we can gain to give distinctness to events of a distant age and circumstances widely different from our own. But at the same time there is a danger in this popular realism. We must not rest in the surface, nor let the form obscure the idea. We must take earnest heed lest that which appeals to the senses or to the imagination usurp the place of the spiritual truth. If under one aspect Christ's earthly life was a life of humiliation, we must remember that even in this He manifested His glory to those who had eyes to see, that the cloud which veiled it came from man's weakness and man's unbelief, that never for one moment did He cease to be the Son of GOD,
John i. 3f. *the Word, through Whom all things were made, and in Whom all things were life.*

Bearing then this central Truth in mind we go on to confess that we *believe in Jesus Christ... Who was conceived by the Holy Ghost, born of the Virgin Mary, suffered under Pontius Pilate, was crucified, dead and buried.*

In the earliest Creeds this article was much

less full. It was not till the seventh century that every element was combined in the form of words which we habitually repeat. For so it is in the order of Providence that we learn by slow experience what points in the one truth require to be emphasised, what details are fruitful for the guidance and support of life. But as the record now stands in a bold outline, which we fill up instinctively from the Gospels, we feel at once what a solemn picture it gives us of a human life, of a human life freely offered for men: 'Conceived, born, suffered, crucified, dead, buried.' Each word marks a crisis in the sacrifice, and helps us to apprehend its completeness. GOD by the working of the Holy Spirit united Himself with man. *The Word became flesh*, and took to Himself under the conditions of human birth our nature and our lot: so Christ was 'conceived' and 'born.' For Christ that lot of man can be briefly summed up in the phrase 'He suffered,' suffered from first to last, even while He grew in favour with GOD and man, as seeing the disharmony between 'His Father' and 'His brethren.' He suffered and He endured the cross, the uttermost shame of suffering, being made an outcast from His own Gal. iii. 13. people who were by calling the people of GOD: 'He was crucified.' In that most terrible form He bore the last issue of sin, though He

v. knew no sin: 'He died.' And He received the last tribute of love from friends who had ceased to hope: 'He was buried.' Step by step we follow the history, and as we reverently ponder it we learn to look to Christ as the One Divine centre of humanity as created: to look to Him as the Redeemer and Restorer of man fallen: we learn to meditate on the Incarnation in itself; and on the sorrows by which it was actually encompassed. We learn something of the lesson of Christ's humanity, something of the lesson of Christ's sufferings. These are the two main lessons of this section of our Creed which we must seek to master.

The lesson of Christ's humanity. Christ was not only truly man, with body, soul, and spirit, in each of which He suffered, by hunger and weariness and pain, by grief and anger, by desolation: He was also and is perfectly man, and He was and is representatively man.

It is not necessary now to dwell on the first of these statements that Christ was truly man. This is written plainly in the whole record of His work. But the two latter thoughts require some explanation; for we must grasp them firmly if we are to understand the power and the promises of the Gospel.

Christ was and is perfectly man. For us humanity is broken up into fragments by sex, by race, by time, by circumstance. From the beginning its endowments were not unequally divided between man and woman, whose differences are essential to the true idea of the whole. And we can see that countless nations and ages have not yet exhausted the manifold capacities of manhood and womanhood under the varied disciplines and inspirations of life. Again and again even in our own experience some new flash of courage or wisdom or patience or tenderness goes to brighten the picture of man's completed and real self. But in Christ there are no broken or imperfect lights. In Him everything which is shewn to us of right and good and lovely in the history of the whole world is gathered up once for all. Nothing limits His humanity, but the limits proper to humanity itself. Whatever there is in man of strength, of justice, of wisdom: whatever there is in woman of sensibility, of purity, of insight, is in Christ without the conditions which hinder among us the development of contrasted virtues in one person. Christ belongs peculiarly to no one people, to no one time. And conversely, if there be aught that is noble in the achievements or in the aspirations of any people or of any time, it finds a place in His sympathy and strength from His example.

This truth is at present of vital importance.

v. There are those even among ourselves who look only on the sterner side of the Lord's nature, and then transfer to His Virgin Mother, or to Saints, all the attributes of compassion and mercy which attract sin-stricken souls. There are those again who lose themselves in the contemplation of these softer traits, and in a selfish and fatal indolence forget the stirring claims, the awful Majesty of the King and the Judge. And yet more than this. We are all tempted to look to Christ as He has been recognised in some other circumstances than our own, to perpetuate and to make absolute a type which has been once hallowed: forgetting that He is revealing Himself to us now, shewing to us under the actual conditions of our present life fresh gifts and energies and hopes of our common nature which He has wholly consecrated, and that the test of our faith is that we discern Him as He shews Himself not to others but to us.

Christ, I repeat, was and is perfectly man: He was and is also representatively man. Seeing that He unites in Himself all that is truly manly and truly womanly, undisguised by the accidental forms which belong to some one country or to some one period, everyone can therefore find in Him for his own work union with the eternal. He is,
1 Cor. xv. 45. in the language of St Paul, '*the last Adam,*' '*a*

life giving spirit.' For Him, consciously or unconsciously, all men were looking: to Him all history tended: in Him a higher life had its beginning and its pledge. *Ye shall see*, John i. 51.
He said Himself in answer to the first confession of faith, *the heaven opened and the angels of God ascending and descending upon the Son of man.* And for us the promise has found accomplishment. In Him we are enabled to perceive that the broken unity of earth and heaven has been restored; in Him we are enabled to recognise that the earlier intercourse between the seen and the unseen worlds has been brought to an absolute fulfilment. Christ *the Son of man* has bestowed on the race the gifts which belonged to Him as *the Son of God*.

Thus Christ is representatively man; and it is by fellowship with His human nature, by taking it to ourselves as He offers it, by striving, as we may, to win that which in the end we shall receive freely from His love, that we all can obtain life. This is what He speaks of as '*eating* John vi. 53.
the flesh of the Son of man, and drinking His blood,' making our own, appropriating, using, the virtue of His humanity as He lived for us, the virtue of His humanity as He died for us. In ourselves we are weak, frail, doomed to death. But there is a power of eternal being within our reach, which is sufficient for every man and fitted for

v. each man. Whatever be our capacities and endowments, due, as the case may be, to our birth, our years, our position, our country, they may be all consecrated through Him Who lived perfectly, Who lived representatively, the life of which we each live a little fragment. Whatever may be our failures, our negligences, our ignorances, they
John i. 29. may be all done away in Him, Who bore the sin of the world, and took it away by bearing it.

So we pass from the lesson of Christ's humanity to the lesson of Christ's sufferings. We believe that the Incarnation would have been necessary for the fulfilment of man's destiny even if he had perfectly followed the divine law. The Passion was necessary for the redemption of man fallen. This is a fact to be thought over. The presence of evil amongst us and in us, in its manifold forms of suffering and selfishness and loss and crime, is a reality which no ingenuity can hide or dissemble. Revelation did not cause this terrible affliction, but it shews that it does not belong to the essence of creation or to the essence of man. It shews therefore that it is remediable: that it can be removed from man without destroying his true nature, nay rather that his true nature is vindicated by the removal. The idea of Christ's sufferings, the idea of redemption, presupposes the idea of a

Fall. Such an idea is, I will venture to say, a necessary condition of human hope. No view of life can be so inexpressibly sad as that which denies the Fall. If evil belongs to man as man there appears to be no prospect of relief here or hereafter. Sin, as old poets say, will have an endless progeny of sins. Misery will be as the shadow which we cast when the sun is brightest. There can be nothing in us to drive out that which is part of ourselves. Strict retribution is the only teaching of that invariable sequence which we call law. But the confession of our belief in Christ's sufferings takes us into a new sphere. We embrace effectual forgiveness as the revelation of the Gospel. Christ took to Himself and bore to the grave the uttermost burden of sinful humanity, and, Himself sinless and victorious over death, offers to men fellowship in the fruits of His conquest. How His life and death avails with the Father for us is a question which we have no power to answer. It is enough for us to acknowledge the supreme triumph of divine love from first to last, one will of one GOD reconciling the world to Himself in Jesus Christ, His only Son, our Lord. V. 2 Cor. v. 19.

But while the lesson of Christ's sufferings is thus, from first to last a lesson of conquering love, we must not forget that He did conquer from first to

v. last by suffering. He offers us in the whole history from Bethlehem to Calvary a measure of our need, a measure of sin. Our imagination is too feeble to realise all that that history suggests, but our hearts cannot but be moved by it. Those long years of silent waiting, those long nights of secret prayer, shew us, as we have the will to see, what present human life is, something infinitely deeper and more solemn than impetuous efforts of hasty enthusiasm or bold conflicts in the sight of men. We must win and bring the perfect offering of ourselves before we can rightly do GOD'S work. There is that within us which must be overcome before we can safely encounter foes without. Communion with GOD in the Risen Christ must be maintained by continuous effort if we are to do our work as men.

All this calls for sacrifice, for sacrifice of will, of pleasure, of ease, which finds its motive and its support in Christ's sufferings. It is impossible for us to look to these and suppose that we who bear His name shall not be made partakers of His temptations: unnatural to wish that we who claim the privilege of sons may not
Heb. v. 8. be fashioned in obedience, as He was, by a Father's discipline.

We tremble perhaps as we use the words,

conscious of our besetting weakness, but can the teaching of our Creed mean less? Is it as an idle form that we trace day by day the outline of Christ's work on earth which brings before us as nothing else can do—if we will but in calm waiting allow it to have its effect—the glory of life and the solemnity of life, the double lesson on which we have dwelt, the lesson of Christ's humanity, the lesson of Christ's sufferings: the lesson of His humanity, by which we learn the brotherhood of men, whereby all in due measure through sorrow and effort, through failure and success, contribute to the fulfilment of the idea of creation: the lesson of His sufferings, by which we learn the true nature and inevitable consequences of sin, whereby the glorious light and glad hymn of the Nativity were followed by the great darkness and bitter cry of the Passion? v. John xxi. 22.

GOD grant that we may learn ever more and more—learn for life—these lessons which our Creed teaches us, the lesson of Christ's humanity, Who was truly, perfectly, representatively man: the lesson of Christ's sufferings, Who was a propitiation not for our own sins only but for the whole world. 1 John ii. 2.

As yet, indeed, man's destiny is not visibly fulfilled: the fruits of Christ's victory are not completely gathered: *we see not yet all things put*

v. *under Him, but we* do *see*—and in this vision lies the assurance of every hope—*we* do *see Him Who hath been made a little lower than the angels, even Jesus, because of the suffering of death crowned with glory and honour.*

VI.

HE DESCENDED INTO HELL; THE THIRD DAY HE ROSE AGAIN FROM THE DEAD, HE ASCENDED INTO HEAVEN, AND SITTETH ON THE RIGHT HAND OF GOD THE FATHER ALMIGHTY.

Now hath Christ been raised from the dead, the first-fruits of them that are asleep. For since by man came death, by man came also the resurrection of the dead. For as in Adam all die, so also in Christ shall all be made alive.

1 COR. XV. 20—22.

We behold Him Who hath been made a little lower than the angels, even Jesus, because of the suffering of death crowned with glory and honour, that by the grace of GOD He should taste death for every man.

HEBR. ii. 9.

Wherefore also GOD highly exalted Him, and gave unto Him the name which is above every name; that in the name of Jesus every knee should bow, of things in heaven and things on earth and things under the earth, and that every tongue should confess that Jesus Christ is Lord, to the glory of GOD the Father.

PHIL. ii. 9—11.

Wherefore also He is able to save to the uttermost them that draw near unto GOD through Him, seeing He ever liveth to make intercession for them. For such a high priest became us, holy, guileless, undefiled, separated from sinners, and made higher than the heavens.

HEBR. vii. 25, 26.

IN considering what the Creed teaches us as to VI.
the earthly work of the Lord, we noticed that events which appear to our eyes full of the deepest sorrow and humiliation may yet include at the same time a divine glory, hidden from us because we have at present no power to see it. Thus in the immediate prospect of the betrayal, of the agony, of the Cross, looking at His work accomplished, when Judas had now gone out into night from the circle of the twelve, the Lord summed up His judgment of all in the memorable words *Now is the Son of man glorified.* The glory was John xiii. 31.
present in the very shame; and we can at length see it there. But none the less this glory is presented to us in our Creed in a succession of facts which correspond with the facts of Christ's life of humiliation. As we confess our belief in Jesus Christ Who was conceived, born, suffered, was crucified, dead, and buried: we confess also that *He descended into Hell; the third day He rose again from the dead: He ascended into heaven, and sitteth on the right hand of GOD the*

VI. *Father Almighty.* Step by step we acknowledge in these clauses Christ's entrance into the world of spirit, His new Birth into the fulness of a glorified human Life, His exaltation to the throne of divine Majesty, His present sovereignty.
Hebr. vii. 16. No death, no limit closes any more the energy of an 'indissoluble life.'

But in thinking of these truths we must use great caution. There is, as I said before, a serious danger in the prevailing spirit of realism which leads us to dwell on the outside, the form, the dress of things, to the neglect of the ideas which are thus half-veiled and half-revealed. And this danger besets us in its gravest shape when we endeavour to give distinctness to the unseen world. We transfer, and we must transfer, the language of earth, the imagery of succession in time and space, to an order of being to which, as far as we know, it is wholly inapplicable. We cannot properly employ such terms as 'before' and 'after,' 'here' and 'there,' of GOD or of Spirit. All *is*, is at once, is present, to Him; and the revelations of the Risen Lord seem to be designed in part to teach us that though He resumed all that belongs to the perfection of man's nature, He was not bound by the conditions which we are forced to connect with it.

While then we are constrained to use words of

time and space, and to speak of going up and coming down, of present and future, in regard to the spirit-world, and Christ's glorified Life, we must remember that such language belongs to our imperfect conceptions as we now are, and not to the realities themselves: that we must not be startled if it leads us to difficulties and contradictions: that we must allow no conclusions to be drawn as to the eternal from the phenomena of time. VI.

This is no doubt a difficult demand to make; and it may seem to deprive us of much which brings joy and strength in the trials and sorrows of earthly life. But indeed the gain is worth the effort. If once we can feel that the imagery in which the glories of the world to come are described is only imagery, we can dwell upon it with ever increasing intelligence and without distraction. There is then no monotony in eternal praise, no weariness in unbroken day, when praise is the symbol of a heart conscious of GOD's infinite goodness, and day of the manifestation of His unclouded truth. The gates of pearl and the streets of gold cease to suggest thoughts of costly display and transitory splendour. The soul uses the figures as helps to spiritual aspiration and welcomes their irreconcileable contrasts as warnings against treating them as literal descriptions of

VI. that which it has not entered into the mind of man to conceive. While therefore we hold thankfully and faithfully that the facts of the spiritual world must be described in words borrowed from the material world, which answer to the unseen realities but cannot express them, we are able to consider with fresh confidence, and not altogether in vain, the eternal meaning of Christ's Descent, Resurrection, Ascension, Session in heaven, as these facts are set forth in our Creed. In our confession that Christ *descended into Hell, rose again, ascended into heaven, sitteth on the right hand of God*, we can see perfectness of divine sympathy in every phase of our existence, absolute ennobling for every human power, access to the divine Presence beyond every confinement of sensible existence, assurance of final victory in every conflict with evil.

He descended into Hell, that is, into Hades, into the common abode of departed spirits and not into the place of punishment of the guilty. This clause, as we know, has given occasion to much misunderstanding and superstition. It is not found in the earliest Creeds and it is almost peculiar to the West. But it is not on this account less precious as part of our heritage. As it stands it completes our conception of the Lord's death. To our minds death is the separation of

body and soul. According to this conception Christ VI.
in dying shared to the full our lot. His Body was laid in the tomb. His soul passed into that state on which we conceive that our souls shall enter. He has won for GOD and hallowed every condition of human existence. We cannot be where He has not been. He bore our nature as living: He bore our nature as dead.

So far the interpretation of this clause *He descended into Hell* seems to be clear; and it carries light into the tomb. But more than this we dare not say confidently on a mystery where our thought fails and Scripture is silent. The stirring pictures which early Christian fancy drew of Christ's entry into the prison-house of death to proclaim His victory and lead away the ancient saints as partners of His triumph; or again to announce the Gospel to those who had not heard it, rest on too precarious a foundation to claim general acceptance. We are sure that the fruits of Christ's work are made available for every man: we are sure that He crowned every act of faith in patriarch or king or prophet or saint with perfect joy: but how and when we know not, and, as far as appears, we have no faculty for knowing. Meanwhile we cling to the truth which our Creed teaches us. To the old world, to Jew and Gentile alike—and it is a fact too often

VI. forgotten—'the Under world,' 'Sheol' the place of spirits, was a place of dreary gloom, of conscious and oppressive feebleness. Even this natural fear of the heart Christ has lightened. There is nothing in the fact of death, nothing in the consequences of death, which Christ has not endured for us: *He was buried, He descended into Hades*, the place of spirits.

But it was not possible that He should be
Acts ii. 31. holden of death: *His flesh saw no corruption: His soul was not left in Hades.* And we confess that *the third day He rose again from the dead.* If death, as I said, is presented to us as the separation of soul and body, the Resurrection is the most complete, nay the eternal, union of the
Rom. vi. 9. two. *Being raised from the dead Christ dieth no more.* The human life which He had before lived under the conditions of space and time, of decay and dissolution, was now gained subject to no change and free from the limitations of earth. At the same time nothing was laid aside or lost which belongs to the fulness of our human nature. The Risen Christ could, without derogating from the perfection of His glorified manhood, shew Himself as believers had known Him before, the same in power of quickening and teaching, the same in sovereign authority and tender sympathy, the same in look and voice: the same, and yet such

that these points of identity were recognised as signs of a being, a love, a presence, unspeakably greater, deeper, more universal, than could have been in any way perceived before He had conquered death. In this way the Resurrection of Christ was a revelation to men of that which GOD has prepared for them that love Him. And as we welcome it into our soul it is able, as I have elsewhere endeavoured to point out, to harmonize life, to inspire life, to transform life. VI.

For as we believe that Christ *rose from the dead*, we believe that He bore from the grave the issues, the fruits, not only of His open ministry and of His final Passion, but also of the unnoticed, silent years of obscure discipline and duty, and shewed these in their spiritual meaning. We believe, and come to feel as we look to Christ Risen, that all the seemingly trivial fragments of life have a unity for man who shall die and live through death.

As we believe that Christ *rose from the dead*, we believe that he made plain to us the realities in the midst of which we are, that by laying open the powers of another order He offered us strength for effort, that by the promise of His fellowship He declared the worth of labour. We believe, and come to feel as we look to Christ Risen, that

VI. we have a motive for work prevailing through all disappointment and failure.

As we believe that Christ *rose from the dead*, we believe that He shewed to us, more directly even than by the Incarnation, the union of the two worlds, the seen and the unseen, and taught us not to turn away from earth that we may find heaven, but to behold in earth the scene of a veiled glory. We believe, and come to feel as we
Acts xvii. 28. look to Christ Risen, that here and now we *live and have our being* in GOD.

But these lessons were not finished by the Resurrection. The appearances of Christ during the great forty days, however mysterious, still set Him in connexion with particular places and
John xvi. 7. times. It was therefore *expedient that He should go away* in order that His disciples might feel Him near them always and everywhere. And we acknowledge that this blessing has been given when we say that *He ascended into heaven.*

For, as we have seen, we are not to think of the Ascension of Christ as of a change of position, of a going immeasurably far from us. It is rather a change of the mode of existence, a passing to GOD, of Whom we cannot say that He is 'there' rather than 'here,' of Whom we all can say 'GOD is with me,' and if GOD then Christ Who has ascended to the right hand of GOD.

When therefore we declare our belief in Christ's Ascension, we declare that He has entered upon the completeness of spiritual being without lessening in any degree the completeness of His humanity. The thought is one with which we need to familiarise ourselves. We cannot indeed unite the two sides of it in one conception, but we can hold both firmly without allowing the one truth to infringe upon the other. And as we do so we shall see how the Ascension illuminates and crowns the lesson of the Resurrection; how it brings home to us now all that the Apostles learnt by their companionship with Christ their earthly Teacher, and with Christ their Risen Lord. VI.

By the Ascension all the parts of life are brought together and shewn in the oneness of their common destination.

By the Ascension Christ in His humanity is brought close to every one of us, and the words 'in Christ,' the very charter of our faith, gain a present power.

By the Ascension we are encouraged to look beneath the surface of things to that which makes all things capable of consecration.

We ponder these lessons of the Presence about us and in us of the Ascended Christ all the days to the end of the world, and the sense of our own weakness becomes perhaps more oppressive than

VI. before. Then it is that the last element in our confession as to Christ's work speaks to our hearts. He is not only present with us as Ascended: He is active for us. We believe that He *sitteth on the right hand of* GOD *the Father Almighty.*

These words express under a natural image the three ideas of an accomplished work, of a divine sovereignty, and, by consequence, of an efficacious intercession.

An accomplished work. The image of Christ's Session is that of perfect rest, of rest which answers to the being of GOD 'Who worketh hitherto' without effort and without failure. The sacrifice has been completed, but the fruits of it remain inexhaustible. The purification of sins has been made, but the application of it is for all time.

A divine sovereignty. Priests stand in their ministry. Angels stand before the throne or fall prostrate at the feet of Him Who reigns there. But Christ is King as well as Priest, Son as well
Hebr. i. 3. as servant. He *sitteth at the right hand of* GOD, sharing in the fulness of GOD'S Majesty, *bearing all things,* bearing them to an appointed end, *by the word of His power.*

An efficacious intercession. The love of GOD can know no change. He Who shewed His love in living and dying for us, loves no less now when that Life and Death have passed into triumph. Nay rather, if we dare to follow the course of human feeling, we may think that the joy of gathering the fruits of toil adds intensity to love. VI.

Such appear to be in the briefest summary, the main thoughts which lie in what our Creed teaches us of Christ's Life in the world of Spirit. They furnish abundant material for meditation; and such thoughts of Christ, the Son of man, throned in glory, are fitted to help us in our common duties. As we ponder them they bring His whole work near to us, to each one of us, with an immediate power. They fix our minds not on anything past nor on anything future, but on what is now. They give definiteness to the uttermost aspirations of worship and faith. They enable us to acknowledge, without turning aside from any of the saddest mysteries of earth, how Christ has fulfilled the destiny of man fallen. They enable us, so to sum up all, to enter little by little into the meaning of the apostolic words, to see *Him who hath been made a little lower than the angels, even Jesus, crowned with glory and honour because of the suffering of death*, that the virtue of His redemption may become available universally, *that He may taste death*, not for all but, with a directly personal application, *for every one*.

VII.

FROM THENCE HE SHALL COME TO JUDGE THE QUICK AND THE DEAD.

The Son of man shall come in the glory of His Father with His angels; and then shall He render unto every man according to his deeds.

MATT. xvi. 27.

But when the Son of man shall come in His glory, and all the angels with Him, then shall He sit on the throne of His glory: and before Him shall be gathered all the nations: and He shall separate them one from another, as the shepherd separateth the sheep from the goats.

MATT. xxv. 31, 32.

Wherefore, receiving a kingdom that cannot be shaken, let us have grace, whereby we may offer service well-pleasing to GOD with reverence and awe.

HEBR. xii. 28.

Behold, He cometh with the clouds; and every eye shall see Him, and they which pierced Him; and all the tribes of the earth shall mourn over Him. Even so, Amen.

APOC. i. 7.

WE have considered what the Creed teaches us of the Lord's Life on earth, and of His Life in the spirit-world, how He has fulfilled the destiny of man, of man fallen, Himself sinless, through suffering. But we do not rest here. As yet the issue of His work is not made plain. We still look for that final revelation in which the Life of earth and the Life of heaven shall be revealed in their unity. Therefore we add to our belief in the Incarnation, the Passion, the Resurrection, the Ascension, the Session of Christ at the right hand of God, the confession that *from thence He shall come to judge the quick and the dead.*

No one can study the New Testament without feeling that the thought of Christ's Return was everywhere present and powerful in the first age. In the Gospels and in the Apocalypse, in the Acts and in the Epistles, the same hope is the subject of promise, of exhortation, of vision; and I do not think that it would be possible to find any other special doctrine of Christianity which is not only affirmed but affirmed in the same language by

VII. St Paul and St James, by St Peter and St John. The return of Christ to judgment was the subject on which St Peter spoke when the Jewish multitude was astonished at the first apostolic miracle after the day of Pentecost: it was the subject on which St Paul spoke when he first passed over into Macedonia and his enemies accused him of preaching 'another king than Caesar.' It seems to rise uppermost in the minds of the apostles when they are most deeply moved themselves and when they wish to move others most deeply. It is as they declare it the sufficient motive for patience in affliction and the end of expectation in the presence of triumphant evil.

And more than this: the hope of Christ's Return was not only general in the first age: the Return was looked for at once. From Jerusalem and Corinth the same voice came that 'the time was at hand,' even as when the Baptist heralded Christ's ministry. The dawn of an endless day was held to be already breaking after a weary night; and while St Paul reproved the error of those at Thessalonica who neglected the certain duties of life that they might, as they fancied, watch better the spread of the heavenly glory, he confirmed the truth which they had misinterpreted.

With us it is far otherwise. A few enthusiasts

from time to time bring the thought of Christ's Return into prominence, but for the most part it has little influence upon our hearts and minds. We have, I think, no definite idea as to what the article of our Creed means by which we profess our belief in it. We acknowledge generally, in a vague manner, that we shall severally render an account of our doings, but we do not look beyond this either in hope or fear to any manifestation of judgment in the world. VII.

And it is to this judgment of the world that the Creed especially directs our attention. For we cannot but notice that in the teaching of Scripture the earth where we suffer and toil is presented as the scene of a universal revelation of Christ's sovereignty; that He enters again into the conditions of human life; that all men are affected by His coming; that His coming is something infinitely more, though it includes this, than the just retribution of individuals.

In this respect there can be no question as to the natural meaning of the language of the New Testament. But it has been said that experience has shewn that the apostolic expectations were mistaken: that they looked in vain, however confidently, for Christ's immediate Return: that we must take warning from their disappointment against indulging in visionary and vain hopes.

VII. I say nothing on the general character of such rash conclusions. I readily admit that there may have been self-willed believers in the first age, as there are in all ages, who boldly determined how Christ should return and how He should establish His Sovereignty. So it was before Christ's first Coming. Such men were indeed disappointed; and, as we see from the Epistle to the Hebrews, they found it hard to submit their fancies to God's will. But their errors, their mistaken and defeated hopes, alter nothing in the fulfilment of the divine counsel. The apostles looked for Christ, and Christ came most truly in the life-time of St John. He founded His immovable kingdom. He gathered before Him, *seated upon the throne of His glory*, the nations of the earth, old and new, and passed sentence upon them. He judged, in that shaking of earth and heaven, most truly and most decisively the living and the dead. He established fresh foundations for society and a fresh standard of individual worth. The fall of Jerusalem was for the religious history of the world an end as complete as death. The establishment of a spiritual Church was a beginning as glorious as the Resurrection.

The apostles, I repeat, looked for Christ's coming in their own generation, and Christ came. The form of His Coming, His Coming to judgment,

at that crisis is a lesson for all time. As we study VII.
it we can learn part at least of the meaning of our present faith, that He shall come again. We see in that Coming the type and the promise of other Comings through the long ages, till the earthly life of humanity is closed. We see in it the signs of a divine Presence which is laid open in the great crises of social movement. We see in it the assurance that the world is not left unvisited by Him Who died for it; and we take courage at the sight.

For it is at once obvious that the Coming of
Christ is not one but manifold. *I will not leave* John xiv.
you desolate—orphans—He said Himself—*I come* 18.
to you. The conviction that this is so gives a new significance to the past and to the future. We look back, and we may without presumption recognise Comings of Christ in earlier centuries of Christendom. We look forward, and with patient confidence we rest in the knowledge that in due time He will shew His purpose and His power to those who love Him.

At the foundation of the Byzantine Empire in the fourth century, at the conversion of the Northern nations in the eighth century, at the birth of Modern Europe in the thirteenth century, at the re-birth of the old civilisation in the sixteenth century, Christ came as King and Judge.

VII. He came, and we can see that He came, at the time when Athanasius, the champion of the East, vindicated the supreme independence of the Faith, and Augustine the champion of the West, affirmed the world-wide embrace of the Church.

He came, and we can see that He came, at the time when the Irish Columban offered to the barbarian warriors the virtues of an unseen power stronger than the arm of flesh, and our own English Boniface sealed by a fearless death a life of victorious sacrifice.

He came, and we can see that He came, at the time when the Italian Francis of Assisi claimed once more for the poor their place in the Church beside emperors and popes and nobles, and taught the love of GOD and the love of man in the universal language of his age.

He came, and we can see that He came, at the time when men as far apart as Loyola and Philip Neri, Luther and Calvin, Colet and Cranmer, shewed in many parts and with many failures that Christ claims and satisfies the individual power of every man.

On each of these occasions new thoughts, new principles, new estimates of things, entered into the world, and remain still to witness to their divine origin. The successive spiritual revolutions were not at once recognised or understood. Christ moved among men and they did not know Him. But meanwhile believers were confessing their faith, as we do, that He should come again to judge the quick and the dead; and we now rejoice to acknowledge that their faith was not in vain though it was confirmed in ways which had not been foreseen.

The wider range of our vision enables us now to recognise these manifold Comings of Christ already accomplished, and we may be most thankful for such teaching of experience, but we do not rest in them. We take the great thought that this world in which we work, with all its sorrows and sins, with all its baffled hopes and unworthy ambitions, is the scene of a divine government. We take the thought, and therefore we believe that Christ has not yet revealed the fulness of His power or uttered the last voice of His judgment. We still say, as we look often with sad hearts on what man has made of man, upon the terrible disproportion between human capacities and human achievements, that He who lived for us and died for us and ascended for us shall come again to judge the quick and the dead; and the confession, if we enter into its meaning, is sufficient to bring back trust.

Perhaps we need the encouragement more than we know. For there are abundant signs of

VII. change about us now. New truths are spreading widely as to the methods of GOD'S working, as to our connexions one with another and with the past and with the future. Through these, as I believe, Christ is coming to us, coming to judge us, and His Coming must bring with it trials and (as we think) losses. Every revelation of Christ is through fire, the fire which refines by consuming all that is perishable. It may then be that we, to our bitter loss, shall fail like those of earlier times to read our lesson as it is given. It may be, the Spirit helping us, that we shall in part interpret it and use it for our inspiration and guidance. It may be at least that we shall gain a living assurance that divine powers are working about us, and a divine purpose going forward to its end, and a divine judgment passing into infallible execution: a living assurance that the article of our Creed which we are considering is not for the past only or for the future only, but for the present too: a living assurance that we may gain strength in the performance of our every-day duties, in the study of the world about us, from knowing that Christ shall come again, is coming again, to judge the quick and the dead.

This aspect of Christ's Coming, the truthful and reverent recognition of His manifestations in history and in society, is of the highest moment

to us now. I have dwelt upon it because it is VII.
often overlooked. But it does not include the whole view of the truth of our Creed. The reality and the meaning of these Comings are clear to faith, but like the Presence of Christ Himself they are hidden from the world. None but believers saw the Risen Christ during the forty days: none but believers see Christ in the great changes of human affairs. But beyond all these preparatory Comings there is a day when *every eye* Apoc. i. 7.
shall see Him, and they also which pierced Him. In that Coming, that Manifestation, that Presence, the first Coming on earth and the later Comings in history shall be shewn in their full import. Then all things, our actions and ourselves, shall be seen as they are, seen by ourselves and seen by others. Then the whole course of life, the life of creation, of humanity, of men, will be laid open, and that vision will be a Judgment beyond controversy and beyond appeal.

It is a judgment universal and personal. In its universal aspect it is the supreme declaration of the truth that there is an end, a goal for creation, a purpose to be fulfilled, a will to be accomplished. We, who see but small fragments of social movement which distract and engross us, are apt to regard history as an aimless succession of changes. Such would be the judgment which

VII. a being of narrower faculties might form from observing a few days or hours of our individual lives. But from time to time revolutions, which are seen to be the intelligible results of the past, reveal the reality of a law of progress in the life of humanity. By the revelation of the final Judgment we are enabled to see that for mankind as for men severally there is an appointed close to earthly work.

The Judgment is personal also. And in this connexion we must master the thought which has been expressed before that the judgment of Christ, the Son of man, is the revelation of things as they are. His judgment does not change the judged: it simply shews them. It is not, as far as we can conceive, a conclusion drawn from the balancing of conflicting elements or a verdict upon a general issue. The judgment of GOD is the perfect manifestation of truth. The punishment of GOD is the necessary action of the awakened conscience. The judgment is pronounced by the sinner himself and he carries out inexorably his own sentence. In our present state a thousand veils hide from us the motives, the thoughts, the conditions which give their real character to men and the conduct of men. We judge of others by what we can see in them: and, what is more perilous still, we are tempted to judge of ourselves by what others can see in us. But in the perfect light of Christ's Presence everything will be made clear in its essential nature, the opportunity which we threw away, and knew that we threw away, with its uncalculated potency of blessing, the temptation which we courted in the waywardness of selfish strength, the stream of consequence which has flowed from our example, the harvest which others have gathered from our sowing. VII.

We know our own hearts imperfectly; but is there one of us whom the thought of this revelation does not fill with contrition?

Our imaginations are dull; but is there one of us who can imagine keener suffering than to see the glory for which we were made and feel that we have sacrificed our birthright?

How this last Coming of Christ to judgment shall be accomplished, which reveals the world to itself, we know not and it is idle to speculate. But for each one of us death is its symbol. For each one of us that solemn coming, which seals our earthly work, is in a most real sense the vision of GOD, instantaneous and age-long, the vision in His light of ourselves.

So it is then, to sum up what has been said, that we confess our belief that Christ shall come again to judge both the quick and the dead: we

VII. believe that He will come socially in the secret spiritual forces which mould kingdoms and churches, and at last with open majesty; we believe that He will come personally in those inner flashes which shew us for a moment the very truth of things, and at last in that supreme hour when He will take account of our finished service. And when we reflect upon the confession we know that it answers to the noblest ideal of life. It declares that there is a purpose in the course of history and in the possibilities of our little parts: that we may look in both for intelligible tokens of the divine will: that it is our duty to lift our eyes to the end when the full work of the Saviour shall be indicated on the scene of His sufferings: that even now we are charged and enabled to find an eternal element underlying the commonest occupations, something which we shall once see as it appears to Him Whose we are and Whom we serve.

Our eyes are dim and our hearts are cold. We fancy that that is far off which is about our feet. We treat as a thought almost indifferent that which is a revelation of the issues of life. This article of our Creed helps us to see things more justly and to cherish greater hopes. An old Gentile writer said, feeling after the truth, 'All things are full of gods': we know that 'all things are full of God,' and that His Presence shall hereafter be made clear, clear in the world at large, clear in our own souls, clear with the manifestation of perfect righteousness and with the consequence of inevitable retribution: VII.

For the Son of man shall come in the glory of His Father with His angels, and then He shall reward every man according to his doing.

Verily I say unto you—the words of the Lord which follow have, I believe, a most certain application to ourselves—*There be some of them that stand here which shall not taste of death till they see the Son of man coming in His kingdom.*

VIII.

I BELIEVE IN THE HOLY GHOST.

The Comforter, even the Holy Spirit, whom the Father will send in My name, He shall teach you all things, and bring to your remembrance all that I said unto you.

JOHN xiv. 26.

But when the Comforter is come, whom I will send unto you from the Father, even the Spirit of truth, which proceedeth from the Father, He shall bear witness of Me.

JOHN xv. 26.

Howbeit when He, the Spirit of truth, is come, He shall guide you into all the truth: for He shall not speak from Himself; but what things soever He shall hear, these shall He speak: and He shall declare unto you the things that are to come. He shall glorify Me: for He shall take of mine, and shall declare it unto you. All things whatsoever the Father hath are mine: therefore said I, that He taketh of mine, and shall declare it unto you.

JOHN xvi. 13—15.

And in like manner the Spirit also helpeth our infirmity: for we know not how to pray as we ought; but the Spirit Himself maketh intercession for us with groanings which cannot be uttered; and He that searcheth the hearts knoweth what is the mind of the Spirit, because He maketh intercession for the saints according to the will of GOD.

ROM. viii. 26, 27.

WE now reach the third division of the Creed. VIII.
We have declared our belief in GOD, the Father, the Ruler and the Maker of all things; and in His only Son Jesus Christ our Lord, Who by taking man's nature upon Him has re-united man to GOD and fulfilled potentially the destiny of creation. As following on this we declare our belief in the Holy Spirit; and so complete the confession of our faith in GOD, our Maker, Redeemer, Sanctifier, One GOD.

In the remaining clauses of the Creed the action of the Holy Spirit is considered in its typical forms, in relation to the society and to the individual, and in its final issue. Because we believe in the Holy Spirit, we believe that there is a Holy Catholic Church and a Communion of Saints, a Church visible and invisible, reaching through all time and to all rational beings. We believe that there is for each one of us a forgiveness of sins and a resurrection of the body, the possibility, that is, of the vision of GOD and the preservation of all that we truly

VIII. are. We believe that there is beyond all the shows and shadows of time, all the changes which make up earthly life, a life eternal, a life in the open Presence of GOD, a life which is the knowledge of GOD.

These special articles of our faith we must reserve for later consideration. I wish now to notice some of the thoughts which are suggested by the general confession: *I believe in the Holy Ghost.* The confession is indeed the confession of a truth which is characteristic of our Christian Creed. We are all now living under that dispensation which is essentially the dispensation of the Spirit. Our whole attitude towards the facts of life is determined by the devout conviction with which we hold it.

The belief in the Holy Spirit is, I say, characteristic of our Christian Creed. The Spirit of GOD appears in the Old Testament as the symbol of the divine energy. He is not yet made known as a distinct Person with Whom man can hold communion, though the scope of the energy foreshadows the nature of the Person. This Spirit it was which brooded over chaos at the Creation: this it was which was breathed into Adam when he became a living soul: this it was by which Moses and Joshua led the people of Israel into the promised land: this it was by which judges wrought deliverance, kings reigned, prophets spoke. Order, life, guidance, truth came from the Spirit of God. But as yet He was not specially revealed as the Holy Spirit. Holiness was seen as the attribute of a Divine Ruler, and not as the essence of a Divine Sanctifier. The Lord of hosts declared Himself as the Holy One of Israel; but in the language of St John *the Spirit was not yet given, because Jesus was not yet glorified.* The Spirit was in the fulness of the Divine Nature, but not in that personal relation with the Church and with the believer which followed on the exaltation of the Saviour.

VIII.

Yet see Ps. li. 11; Is. lxiii. 10 f.

John vii. 39.

Even in the New Testament the revelation of the Holy Spirit is gradual. That which is promised in the Gospels becomes fact in the Acts and the Epistles. At the Incarnation, the Baptism, the Temptation, the Spirit Who was active at the Creation of man was revealed as active at his new creation. But it was not till the full consequences of sin had been borne, and death had been conquered, and humanity had been raised in the Son of man to the right hand of God, that the rushing wind and fiery tongues told outwardly, at the festival of the gathered harvest, of the fulfilment of the promise of the Father. Then first, in virtue of Christ's finished work and in Christ's name, God took up His dwelling, if I may

VIII. so speak, not in the flesh only but in men. The primæval curse of Babel was reversed in the freedom of spiritual utterance; and Galilæan peasants proclaimed intelligibly to the collected nations a universal Gospel. This descent, this incorporation, of the Spirit was in some sense, a second Divine Nativity, the birth of the Church, 'Christ's Body,' the beginning of the order under which we live, the manifestation of that Power which is around us and in us, in Whose help alone lies all our strength, in Whose presence alone lies all our safety. Under this aspect the book of the Acts is the Gospel of the Holy Spirit, the typical record of His action. There we see how, at each stage in the building of the Church, the personal direction of the Spirit rules the conduct of its earthly founders. The voice of the Spirit shewed to St Philip, to St Peter, to St Paul the widening limits of their teaching, and in some cases the very details of their fortunes.

The veil which was thus raised for a brief space from the processes of life in the growth of the Church of GOD has now again fallen over them. We can no longer infallibly interpret the method in which the Spirit works, but we rest in the assurance that He is working. We look back to the first Christian Pentecost and know that we enjoy a special manifestation of His Being which was not made in times of old. As we acknowledge the blessing we see how the whole cycle of man's knowledge of GOD has been completed, and how the fruits of GOD's love are brought into the life of men. We see how GOD has been pleased to make Himself known successively as Father, Son, and Holy Spirit, in revelations which correspond with the progress of His people, and no less, as we are taught to believe, with the mysteries of His own Being. We see how the results of the Incarnation are realised in the Church, and in men, by the abiding ministry of the Paraclete. VIII.

For the Paraclete, the Holy Spirit, is sent in Christ's name. This truth is vital for the understanding of our faith in the Holy Ghost. Even as Christ came in His Father's name, working by His power and therein revealing His character, so the Spirit comes in Christ's name, making known through the ages, as the experience of men grows richer and their powers gain strength by discipline, the infinite truths of the Incarnation which Christ's 'name' embodies. The dispensation of the Spirit is, in other words, the revelation of Christ, the Son of GOD and the Son of man. The promise is for us and for all time. The assurance of the promise is the living hope of the Church; and human history, the history of

John xiv. 26.

VIII. each soul and the history of all nations, furnishes the element through which the Spirit reveals Him.

The Spirit of truth, Christ Himself said, *shall take of mine and declare it unto you;* and again, *all things whatsoever the Father hath are mine.* So He declares to us the method and the end of that order under which we live. Little by little the Spirit is bringing home the uttermost realities of being, bringing home, that is, Christ and the things of Christ to each man and to all men. He is bringing to light new truths which may minister to the knowledge of Him Who is the Truth. He is ever fashioning for our use, as we gain power to use them, new forms of thought, new modes of worship, new spheres of action. There can be no stationariness where He is present.

Little by little He is giving through manifold discipline perfectness to the individual and unity to the Church. He is enabling us to see through the spontaneous aspirations of men fresh depths of promise in the Gospel of Christ. For if our hearts are moved when statesmen or students speak with glowing hope of the coming union of nations, of the progress of society, of the glory of creation, where shall we find a solid basis for their brilliant structures, except in the work of Christ, in the

Person of Christ, which the Spirit interprets to us? The noblest speculations of men who have not the Faith are thus unconscious prophecies of which the Spirit foreshews the fulfilment: stirring calls to us to make clearer the power of that which we have received: pledges that something is given us to do that the counsel of GOD may be more fully known. VIII.

The dispensation of the Spirit is, I repeat, the revelation of Christ. And how do we stand towards it? We often think, I fancy, as we linger over the pages of the Bible, that if GOD shewed Himself to us, as to patriarchs and lawgivers of old; if Christ taught in our streets, as He taught in Nazareth or Capernaum; we should penetrate through every disguise in which the Divine form was shrouded and welcome the words of life with the enthusiasm of complete devotion. We forget that the power to see GOD and to hear Him belongs by an inalienable gift to the soul which loves Him. Meanwhile GOD is reasoning with us with a voice as clear as that which sounded in the still evening through the trees of Eden. One is standing over us—over each one of us—with love as watchful as that of Jesus in the home at Bethany. But too swiftly the unbidden voice dies away in our hearts: the startling consciousness is lost; and we believe that we are alone.

VIII. We often think, again, that if we had received any direct promise, any clear charge, from God, like Abraham, or David, or Peter, we should be ready to go forth as wanderers, as leaders, as martyrs, strong in the might of that eternal assurance, of that irrevocable commission, strong in spite of loneliness, strong in spite of the burden of besetting sin, strong in spite of the remembrance of past faithlessness. In all this we vainly wish for the signs of another age now at length made luminous; and we forget that the seal of the Spirit is on our foreheads, and that we have only to claim our heritage and go forth to share in a victory which has been already won. John xvi. 33.

The inspiration, the personal call, the personal consecration are all for us if we hold fast our Faith.

I believe in the Holy Ghost. He who is able to make the confession stands as a listener to a divine message. For him there is a meaning, however little he may yet be able to grasp it, in the sequences of natural law, in the confused conflicts of empires, in the distresses and anxieties and sordid cares of society. In the confidence of his faith he will not close the least avenue through which one word of God may come to him. In the vigour of his hope he will bear the season of silence when searching finds no answer. In the breadth of his love he will welcome as fellow-helpers those who serve unconsciously the creed which they deny. VIII.

I believe in the Holy Ghost. He who is able to make the confession has found a divine Friend. For him the Spirit is not an influence, an energy, of One far off, but a present Comforter Whom Christ has sent to fulfil His work, a present Guide ready to lead him into all the Truth, a present Advocate waiting to gain acceptance for the deep sighings of the heart before the throne of GOD. So it is that Scripture speaks of His relation to us: so it is that we can understand how His Presence among men is dependent on the exaltation of Christ in His human nature to the right hand of the Father.

I believe in the Holy Ghost. He who is able to make the confession recognises the action of One who is moulding his single life. Each believer is himself a temple to be prepared for the Master's dwelling. The same Spirit Who shapes the course of the whole world hallows the soul which is offered to Him for a divine use. The Christian believer is in one sense alone with GOD, and GOD alone with him. He has a work to do, definite, individual, eternal, through the ordinary duties and occupations and trials of common business; and this the Spirit sent in Christ's name, bringing to him the virtue of Christ's humanity, will help him to perfect.

VIII. *I believe in the Holy Ghost.* Life is indeed full of mysteries to which we can give no interpretation, of griefs to which we can gain no present remedy. I have no will to extenuate them. Nay rather we must feel them deeply if we are to know GOD; and then the faith in the personal help of the Holy Spirit—the complement of the Incarnation—is sufficient for our needs. The prayer of the warrior of old time bewildered by the darkness was: 'Give light and let me die.' We can say: 'Help us to live and the light will come,' come through life itself.

So may we cherish each impulse towards good as the direct inspiration of GOD which bears with it the assurance of its accomplishment. So may we watch the signs of an unseen power moulding us by gentlest influences to the pattern of a divine likeness. So may we have our eyes opened to see a heavenly order slowly fulfilled about us. In that conviction, in that experience, in that vision, we shall work on with the certain knowledge that each effort is blessed by Him who inspired it. Each age, each heart, has its own questionings, but Christ's words are addressed to every age and to every heart: they can never want their accomplishment: *The Paraclete, even the Holy Spirit, whom the Father will send in My name, He shall teach you all things.*

IX.

THE HOLY CATHOLIC CHURCH: THE COMMUNION OF SAINTS.

Where two or three are gathered together in my name, there am I in the midst of them.

MATT. xviii. 20.

This is that which hath been spoken by the prophet Joel;

And it shall be in the last days, saith GOD,
I will pour forth of my Spirit upon all flesh:
And your sons and your daughters shall prophesy,
And your young men shall see visions,
And your old men shall dream dreams.

ACTS ii. 16 f.

He put all things in subjection under His feet, and gave Him to be head over all things to the church, which is His body, the fulness of Him that filleth all in all.

EPH. i. 22 f.

So then ye are no more strangers and sojourners, but ye are fellow-citizens with the saints, and of the household of GOD, being built upon the foundation of the apostles and prophets, Christ Jesus Himself being the chief corner stone; in whom each several building, fitly framed together, groweth into a holy temple in the Lord; in whom ye also are builded together for a habitation of GOD in the Spirit.

EPH. ii. 19 ff.

WE have seen that the general expression of our belief in the Holy Ghost, the Spirit of Truth, the Advocate sent by the Father in Christ's name, to bring home to us ever more and more of the meaning of the Incarnation, is defined in detail by a confession of our belief in His action on the whole Christian Body and upon individual Christians. Because we believe in the Holy Ghost, because we throw ourselves with complete trust upon the efficacy of His divine influence, of His invisible Presence, we believe that there is a society in which it finds embodiment. We believe that there are men in whom it finds due scope for its working. We believe that there is a life, a life eternal, which corresponds with the fulness of its energy. We have then to notice now the first of these three articles of our faith. We believe that there is a *Holy Catholic Church*, a *Communion of Saints:* or, in other words, a Body of Christ seen and unseen, by which the Truth is on the one side presented IX.

IX. outwardly before the world and on the other brought home with concentrated power to the souls of believers. We believe that there is a *Holy Catholic Church.* We do not say, you will observe, that we believe in it as we believe in the Persons of the Godhead. We do not say that we believe it as speaking with a clear, authoritative voice. We say that we believe in the reality of its existence; we believe, in spite of all appearances, that it *is.* This conviction is a work of faith. It must be so. We see the many separate Churches: we mourn over the grievous failures and sins of Christians, over our own failures and sins: we acknowledge in this Communion and in that the declaration and the power of some part of the universal Gospel. All this is matter of experience, of sight. But beyond this separation, this imperfection, this fragmentariness, we believe, though we cannot see, that there is a Church, One, Holy, Catholic, the Body of Christ, through which He is slowly revealing Himself in many parts and advancing to a complete sovereignty over the world. This is what our Creed teaches us to believe. And as we hold the belief more firmly, as we come to understand better the promises which the confession carries with it, our separate labours will be made more hopeful, more humble and more intense.

IX.

We believe, I say, that there is *one* Church, the Body of which Christ is the Head. If we look only at the outside of things there is nothing to justify the bold avowal. The words have been repeated for more than 1500 years, and that whole interval is darkened by the record of corruptions and revolutions, of schisms and heresies. The words are repeated now by different societies throughout the world which refuse to one another the visible symbols of friendship. Can we then—let us ask ourselves the question plainly—can we profess our belief that there is *one* Church when we recall the divisions of Christendom, as we must do in sorrow of heart? *One* Church when rival bodies challenge our allegiance and compass sea and land to make a proselyte? *one* Church when a death-like torpor has fallen over the East, and the farthest West is too often hurried away by a wild fanaticism? *One* Church when each noblest Communion is itself broken into parties eager to narrow the limits of their inheritance by the peculiarities of their own opinions? *one* Church when on this side and on that we are answered by anathema if we bear the greeting of peace? Yes, I believe that there is one Church though I cannot see its unity, in spite of lethargy and unchastened zeal, in spite of the private creeds and reckless judgments which seem to separate what God has joined together.

IX. In this respect the trial of our faith is no new thing. There never was an epoch since the Church spread beyond Jerusalem when the 'one Body of Christ' was one in visible uniformity or even one in perfect sympathy. Time has indeed hardened and multiplied the differences between the several parts into which the Church is divided; but it is possible to trace already in the apostolic age the essential features of those divisions over which we grieve. And if we look forward to the fulfilment of the great promise which gladdens the future, it is not that there shall ever be, as we wrongly read, 'one fold,' one outward society of Christians, gathered in one outward form, but, what answers more truly to present experience
John x. 16. and reasonable hope, *one flock and one shepherd.*

And in the meantime, let us rate the differences of Christians as highly as we will, there yet remains a common faith in the presence of which they are almost as nothing. He who believes, to take the ground of the apostolic message on the day of Pentecost, that Christ rose from the dead, he who is baptized into Him, he who rejoices though trembling in the pledge of a glorified humanity, is divided from the world without by an interval as wide as that between life and death.
Eph. iv. 4, 5. In this *one faith, one baptism...one hope of our calling,* lies a universal fellowship of believers, the symbol and the earnest of the brotherhood of

men, the single truth which taken alone distinguishes for ever Christian from ancient thought. Looking then to this trust in a common redemption, let us hold fast our belief in one Church, in one Body of Christ knit together by the rites which He Himself appointed, one in virtue of the One Spirit Who guides each member severally as He will, of the One Saviour Who fulfils Himself in many ways, of the *One GOD and Father of all, Who is over all and through all and in all.* IX. Eph. iv. 6.

But Faith does not rest here: it holds a second paradox. We believe in the unity of the Church. We believe also in its holiness. We believe this again notwithstanding the sad witness of sight. The weaknesses and the crimes of Christians are a commonplace of our enemies. We can have no desire to excuse them. But these individual failures do not alter the character, the testimony of the body. *Ye are clean,* John xiii. 10. the Lord said to the twelve on the eve of the Passion, *but not all:* they were holy taken together though Judas was among them. And the Church as a society asserts unfalteringly the claims of the Gospel though the message may often be the condemnation of those who bear it. The ideal is firmly held forth through all disasters. And this maintenance of a great faith is a power of life. We read that when Rome had received

IX. the heaviest defeat in her long history, the citizens went forth in a body to meet the conquered general and thanked him because he had not despaired of the commonwealth. That spirit was the life of the old republic. And the Christian Church, wearied and betrayed by men, does not despair of humanity. By that spirit she vindicates her life. She offers to all without reserve and without doubt the calling to holiness and the assurance that the call can be obeyed.

Nor has the call ever been wholly without effect. To those who look a little below the surface the darkest times furnish examples of consecrated lives which visibly embody the teaching of the Church. We have all known such: these openly shew forth what the will of GOD is, and present the first-fruits of its fulfilment. They are felt to be truly representative of the temper and of the power of the Faith. They exhibit what is the idea of the Christian society, and they recognise their dependence upon its institution.

Thus the Church is holy in regard to its unchanging spirit: holy in regard to those who realise its conception. It is holy also in regard to its institutions. One thought runs through all the services not only of our own Communion but, I will venture to say, of all Christian Communions, even that of the devotion, the transfiguration of life. However true it may be that we fail to enter consciously into the meaning of all the rites in which we share, their testimony is not altogether lost. No one can fail to feel upon reflection how the two Sacraments speak of death and life through death, of life given and life received again. And even before we realise their power by thought, they create by their very existence a kind of spiritual atmosphere about us which is independent of ourselves. They constrain us to consider our destiny, to look beyond earth, to acknowledge that we too have that which must be brought to the presence of GOD. IX.

Grateful therefore for these blessings, for the unceasing voice of a heavenward calling, for the encouragement of Christian lives, for the encompassing influence of Christian services, we can confess, without dissembling the evils about us and in us, that we believe in a Holy Church.

One other title still remains; and if we believe that the Church is one in spite of its outward divisions; if we believe that it is holy in spite of its manifest stains and imperfection; we shall be prepared to understand why we confess that it is catholic, universal. The title was not given to the Church in the Western Creed till the fourth century; and it is itself the monument of a long conflict. The word does not express

IX. simply, as we commonly understand it, the universality of the extension of the Church: it affirms also the universality of the teaching of the Church. The real sign of the supremacy of the Christian society is not that it spreads everywhere but that it embraces the whole truth. This is the sure pledge of the Church's dominion. The Catholic Church welcomes joyfully and ministers openly every treasure of wisdom and knowledge for her children.

The word 'Catholic' is, I have said, the monument of a long conflict. In the first age there were some who shrank from the teaching of St Paul; others who received St Paul only: some who cast aside the Old Testament; others who found in it the complete record of revelation. Slowly and certainly the elements of truth which were disguised in these conflicting and fragmentary views were reduced to harmony. Slowly and certainly the full collection of prophetic and apostolic Scriptures was brought perfectly together, and the same epoch saw a Catholic Bible and a Catholic Church.

From that time these two ideas, these two facts, have lain at the foundation of Christendom. The one—the Catholic Bible—furnishes the test of apostolicity for all doctrines: the other—the Catholic Church—adds the materials of life for their embodiment. Both include elements of contrast and therefore of progress. Because the Bible is Catholic, because it includes the complementary aspects of the Faith, it is possible to construct out of it partial schemes which first become perilous when they are treated as complete. Because the Church is Catholic, because, that is, the whole sum of divine truth, the whole sum of all truth, is its heritage, it has always some fresh message to deliver. It offers to each age, to each nation, to each person, what each needs most, and grows stronger as they accept and employ its gifts. For us in our day our belief in the Catholicity of the Church is the assurance of its growth, the assurance that its compass is as wide as the Bible and its energy as manifold as life; that it also, without inconstancy and without change, becomes, in some sense, all things to all men. IX.

But we go yet farther in our confession. The Holy Catholic Church is not only a great fact: it is also a great power: it carries with it an influence not limited by time or space. We are not heirs only of the past; the past lives for us in its spiritual energy. So our Western forefathers added, at the end of the fifth century, a fresh clause to the Creed in order to give clear expression to this characteristic thought,

IX. and taught us to declare our belief in *the Communion of Saints.*

The clause opens new realms of thought to the soul. As we repeat it we seem to enter within the veil. The seen and the unseen, earth and heaven, are united in a spiritual fellowship. Patriarchs and prophets and kings and martyrs, men and angels, are shewn to us in a present connexion with ourselves. The horizon of our hope is indefinitely enlarged. Even though we may be unable as yet to give any definite shape to our intercourse the sense of its reality is ennobling; and as we ponder the fact thus shadowed out we feel something of the infinite depth of life which is contained in the words *I am*
Matt. xxii. 32. *the* GOD *of Abraham and the* GOD *of Isaac and the* GOD *of Jacob.* I *am* the GOD: the existence, the possibility of this divine covenant is the promise of an undying life, a life of which we are made partakers, a life in which men and angels *live unto* GOD.

I believe in *the Holy Catholic Church, the Communion of Saints.* Every article of our Creed is, as we have already seen, a source of strength, an endowment to be put to use. We can all feel how these articles on which we have just touched are fitted to become so. Too often perhaps we make no effort to appropriate their help, though the commonest experience shews what it must be. To belong to a great family, to a great society, to a great nation, is, if rightly viewed, a man's noblest birthright. He whose name is a memorial of past honours, and whose earliest years are spent, as it were, in the light of illustrious deeds: he who has learnt to feel that there is a history in which he has a part and who has rejoiced in the triumphs of a people whose hopes and impulses he shares; must from time to time be raised above all that is selfish and even personal; he must become conscious of the accumulated power with which he is endowed and of the social destiny to which he is called. Let the name be that name which is above every name: let the history be written in every splendid achievement by which the kingdom of GOD has been advanced: let the triumphs be those by which faith through the ages subdues all things to herself: let the fellowship be that of Saints and Confessors; and then we shall understand, dimly it may be but yet so that effort will be kindled with fresh enthusiasm, what our fathers meant when they handed down to us truths which they had proved in actual experience: then we shall say with livelier imagination and fuller heart, each in the prospect of our

IX. little work and with the sense of our peculiar trials, acknowledging that that work is transfigured by a divine consecration and that those trials are conquered by a spiritual sympathy:

I believe in the Holy Catholic Church: I believe in the Communion of Saints.

X.

THE FORGIVENESS OF SINS: THE RESURRECTION OF THE BODY.

Are ye ignorant that all we who were baptized into Christ Jesus were baptized into His death?

If we died with Christ, we believe that we shall also live with Him.

ROM. vi. 3, 8.

Wherefore if any man is in Christ, he is a new creature: the old things are passed away; behold, they are become new.

2 COR. v. 17.

The Lord Jesus Christ...shall fashion anew the body of our humiliation, that it may be conformed to the body of His glory, according to the working whereby He is able even to subject all things unto Himself.

PHIL. iii. 21.

The GOD of peace himself sanctify you wholly; and may your spirit and soul and body be preserved entire, without blame at the coming of our Lord Jesus Christ.

1 THES. v. 23.

WE considered in the last lecture the action x. of the Holy Spirit in the Christian society. We saw that we can without dissembling any of the sad facts of life, the divisions, the crimes, the narrownesses of Christians, yet profess our faith in the real existence of a Church One, Holy, and Catholic; and that the belief is fitted to bring to us thoughts of peace and strength in the course of work which is often clouded by disappointments. We saw that we can, without presuming to define the life of heaven or measure spiritual forces by the conditions of earth, yet profess our faith in the present energy of a Communion of Saints; and that the belief is fitted to bring home to us the manifold powers of divine sympathy when we are distressed by the necessary isolation of much human effort. We have now to notice what our Creed teaches us of the action of the Holy Spirit upon the individual believer: how the Spirit on the one side sanctifies him and so makes

x. him able to behold God; and on the other side how the believer perfectly preserves even in that most awful Presence the fulness of his personal being, body soul and spirit.

I believe, we say, in *the forgiveness of sins.* I believe in *the resurrection of the body.* Here again no less than in our belief in the Church we rise above experience, above sight. We affirm that which nature cannot justify and which still the soul importunately craves after. And in each affirmation we appeal tacitly to the facts of the Lord's Life in confirmation of our faith. The Passion of Christ is for us the seal of forgiveness. The Resurrection of Christ is the pledge of our resurrection.

I believe in *the forgiveness of sins.* Nothing superficially seems simpler or easier than forgiveness. Nothing if we look deeply is more mysterious or more difficult. With men perhaps forgiveness is impossible. For forgiveness is not the careless indifference to wrong by which we seek impunity for our own faults while we lightly regard the faults of others. It is not the complacent bounty of a superior who has a proud satisfaction in giving to others release from small debts. It is not the perfunctory remission of a present penalty which leaves behind unremoved the sense and the contagion of evil. True forgiveness involves two things, a perfect knowledge of the offence, and a perfect restoration of love. In this sense we believe in the forgiveness of sins. 'That which is impossible with men is possible with GOD.' GOD knows, as men cannot know, the nature of sin; and still He offers Himself to us. What that knowledge is, what that love is, is shadowed out for us in the fact that He sent His only Son to be the Saviour of the world: He sent His Son to die that we might live. x.

Nature, I said, knows no forgiveness. With her there is no return of opportunity, no obliteration of the past. The deed done remains while the world lasts. The deed left undone is a blank for ever. There is no exaggeration in the startling thought of a recent writer that it would be possible with powers not different in kind from our own to read backwards in the succession of physical changes the history of our earth, to hear again the last cry of the murdered slave cast into the sea and to look again on the last ripple of the water that closed over him. Each act of man obviously goes on working, and working after its kind, in the doer and in his children's children. So it is also with thought and with feeling. The bad thought once admitted avenges itself by rising again unbidden and unwelcome. The bad feeling once indulged in

x. spreads through the whole character and gives birth to other like passions. Sin in every form is the violation of law, and law inexorably requires its penalty to the uttermost. We need not discuss whether the penalty is retributive or reformatory: it is in the nature of things that it must be paid. That is enough for us. To reason, if we are honest with ourselves, the great mystery of the future is not punishment but forgiveness.

This being so we can understand how the forgiveness of sins was the essential message of the Gospel. The work of Christ which first shewed, as men could see, the nature and the issue of sin shewed also the efficacy and the universality of the divine love. In Christ there was unclouded vision of men's infirmities and unfailing sympathy
Matt. ix. 6. with men. *The Son of man*—because He was Son of man—*had power on earth to forgive sins.* In His own Person He fulfilled the will of God. In His own Person He fulfilled the destiny of man. And whosoever is *in Him* shares the virtue of His Life. By such a union the evil of the past is done away, and the crowning miracle of finite existence is accomplished. By such a union there is true forgiveness of sins. And St John, as if to emphasise the mystery, describes it under a paradox: the
Apoc. vii. 14. redeemed, he says, *washed their robes and made*

them white in the blood of the Lamb—made them x.
white in blood.

We weary ourselves vainly in endeavouring to shape these truths into a system. We have no faculties for such speculations. It is enough for us to rest in the language of the apostles. The blood of Christ—the life of Christ that was wholly rendered, sacrificed to GOD, that so it might be available for others—is the means of our forgiveness, of our access to GOD: repentance and faith are the conditions of that fellowship with Him whereby His sacrifice is effectual for each believer. For, as we have just seen, we must be one with Him—His life must be our life—before His work avails for us. And so it is that 'the remission of sins' has always been connected with Baptism, the sacrament of incorporation. 'We acknowledge one Baptism for the remission of sins' that so the realisation of the atonement may be most vividly connected with the entrance on a new being. And here there is nothing unreal: nothing inconsistent with the purest images which we can form of the justice and holiness of GOD: nothing which is not confirmed by the experience of the human soul as it strives to forgive. The penalty of wrong must be borne; and we are so constituted that we can take another's burden and communicate to him of the

x. fulness of our strength. We can even see in some degree how this outflow of regenerating love transforms the consequences of the past. Such teachings of life are the vantage-ground of faith, and all these faint shadows of an energy in us, partial, isolated, limited, find their substance in Christ,
Matt. viii. 7. Who took upon Him humanity, Who *took our infirmities and bare our sicknesses,* and by bearing removed them, Who gave new life to the sinner by
Col. i. 20. uniting him to Himself, Who *made peace by the blood of His cross, and reconciled all things to God.*

Looking then to that perfect life of the Son of Man, looking to His voluntary endurance of the consequences of sin, being Himself free from all sin, looking to His absolute communion with the Father through life and through death, looking to His love which calls out love, to His word which proclaims rest, we can, in spite of the sternest examples of natural retribution, which cover the whole field of the world, declare our faith in *the forgiveness of sins.*

'So I saw in my dream,' to quote the familiar words of our great English allegory, 'that just as 'Christian came up with the Cross, his burden 'loosed from off his shoulders, and fell from off his 'back and began to tumble, and so continued to 'do, till it came to the mouth of the sepulchre, 'where it fell in, and I saw it no more.' But

when we reflect upon what this forgiveness means: x.
when we consider how profoundly character is influenced by imperfections of nature, by the results of earlier conflicts and defeats, how the man whom we know is identified in part by scars in soul and body, we may ask how he, the friend of our human affection, will survive this glorious change when it is consummated in heaven. Therefore in regarding the future we complete our confession and say: I believe in *the resurrection of the body*, or, as it is in the original without variation, *the resurrection of the flesh*. I believe, that is, that all that belongs to the essence of my person, manifested at present in weakness, marred by the results of many failures, limited by the circumstances of earth, will remain through a change which the imagination cannot realise. I believe that the conflict between the spirit and the flesh which saddens the chequered course of life and adds fresh burdens to memory will not continue for ever. I believe that body soul and spirit, the manifold powers by which I act and feel and think and hold communion with the unseen here in a condition of humiliation, will be preserved entire in the day of the Lord and find a new expression in a condition of glory. I believe that even if depths of life be then opened into which my life will pass, and truths of fellowship be revealed which will

X. outweigh without destroying all sense of separate existence, I—I who have laboured and loved, I who have striven to know the world and man and GOD—shall not be lost, but find the fruit and the meaning of my toil in that living unity to which I shall contribute.

I believe in *the resurrection of the flesh.* But in shaping for ourselves this belief we need to use more than common care lest we allow gross, earthly, thoughts to intrude into a realm where they have no place. The 'flesh' of which we speak as destined to a resurrection is not that material substance which we can see and handle, measured by properties of sense. It represents, as far as we now see, ourselves in our actual weakness, but essentially ourselves. We in our whole being, this is our belief, shall rise again. And we are not these changing bodies which we bear. They alter, as we know, with every step we take and every breath we draw. We make them, if I may so speak, make them naturally, necessarily, under the laws of our present existence. They are to ourselves, to use a bold figure, as the spoken word to the thought, the expression of the invisible.

> For of the soul the body form doth take,
> For soul is form and doth the body make.

When therefore the laws of our existence are

hereafter modified, then we, because we are unchanged, shall find some other expression, truly the 'same' in relation to that new order, because it is not the same as that to which it corresponds in this. x.

All imagery fails in some part or other to present a truth like this. But we should have been spared many sad perplexities, many grievous misrepresentations, if we had clung to St Paul's figure of the seed in looking to our future resurrection. *We sow not*, he tells us, *that body which shall be.* There is then no question here of the regathering of material particles, no encouragement for unsatisfying appeals to GOD'S omnipotence. What St Paul teaches us to expect is the manifestation of a power of life according to law under new conditions. *GOD giveth to every seed a body of its own:* not arbitrarily but according to His most righteous will. The seed determines what the plant shall be but it does not contain the plant. The golden ears with which we trust again to see the fields waving are not the bare grains which were committed to the earth. The reconstruction of the seed when the season has come round would not give us the flower or the fruit for which we hope. Nay rather the seed dies, is dissolved, that the life may clothe itself in a nobler form. True it is that we cannot in

1 Cor. xv. 37 ff.

X. this way escape from a physical continuity; but it is a continuity of life and not of simple reconstruction. And St Paul warns us that the change which we cannot follow is greater than the changes of earth which we can follow: that the development of life goes on: that the manifestation of life takes place, as I said, under new conditions. Everything, he tells us, which characterises a material body, the flower no less than the seed, shall then cease to be. The unbroken continuity shall enter into a new sphere, unaffected by the limitations through which earthly bodies are what they are. *It is sown in corruption: it is raised in incorruption. It is sown in dishonour: it is raised in glory. It is sown in weakness: it is raised in power. It is sown a natural body: it is raised a spiritual body.*

Such a faith as this, even in its necessary vagueness, is sufficient to fill the heart of man. It substitutes for the monotony of continuance the vision of existence infinitely ennobled. It substitutes for the abstract thought of immortality, the rich fulness of a life in which all history and all nature finds its place. It leaves no room for the misgivings which haunt us when we people heaven with creatures of earth. It preserves the chastening thought that we may enter into life incomplete and maimed, if powers of vision or

action or movement, the eye, the hand, the foot, x.
in the language of the Gospels, have been lost because they were not consecrated. It helps us to feel how the forgiveness of sins will restore to men their true selves, disguised and hidden before. In this assurance we can look joyfully upon the removal of all that is transitory, *knowing that we* Hebr. x. 34.
have our own selves for a better possession and an abiding one.

We ask then no more. We define nothing which Scripture has not defined, as to the limits of the place of human repentance or of the form of divine revelation. We acknowledge what we are and were. And therefore we strive, as we have the power, to deepen our sense of sin, to see it as God has shewn it to us in the Mission of His only Son. We strive to apprehend practically the momentous issues of life, the seed out of which the future must grow. We recognise the conditions which must be satisfied in order that we may behold God. We recognise the natural consequences of all action. In the face of this antagonism we turn again, humbled it may be by sharp teachings of experience, to our belief in the Holy Spirit active in the Church, active in the single soul. He is sent to us in Christ's name to accomplish in us Christ's work. The Spirit

x. helpeth our infirmities. The Spirit maketh intercession for us. The Spirit hallows the temple in which He dwells. He who raised up Christ will quicken also our mortal bodies. Believing this we believe also in *the forgiveness of sins* and in *the resurrection of the flesh.*

Believing this we repeat one for another, each for all, the apostle's prayer: *The GOD of peace Himself sanctify you wholly: and may your spirit and soul and body be preserved entire, without blame, at the presence of our Lord Jesus Christ.*

Faithful is He that calleth you Who will also do it.

XI.

THE LIFE ETERNAL.

As it is written,
Things which eye saw not, and ear heard not,
And which entered not into the heart of man,
Whatsoever things GOD *prepared for them that love Him.*

1 COR. ii. 9.

And this is life eternal, that they should know thee the only true GOD, *and Him whom thou didst send, even Jesus Christ.*

JOHN xvii. 3.

And we know that the Son of GOD *is come, and hath given us an understanding, that we know Him that is true, and we are in Him that is true, even in His Son Jesus Christ. This is the true* GOD, *and eternal life.*

1 JOHN v. 20.

And when all things have been subjected unto Him, then shall the Son also Himself be subjected to Him that did subject all things unto Him, that GOD *may be all in all.*

1 COR. xv. 28.

WE close the summary of our belief in the Lord's work by the confession that He will 'come to judge the quick and the dead:' we close the summary of our belief in the Spirit's work by confessing 'the Resurrection of the body.' That universal Judgment, that personal Resurrection, prepare the consummation of all things. We complete our Creed therefore by declaring that we believe in 'the life eternal,' that man made in the image of GOD, and made for GOD, will in due time enter into the life of GOD. XI.

In touching on the doctrine of the Resurrection of the Body—of the Flesh—we saw that there is need of the greatest care lest we should extend to the idea itself the present limitations under which we are forced to think when we endeavour to give a distinct shape to it. The same caution is required in speaking of 'the life eternal.' For us duration, permanence, is

XI. the sign of that which is. We pass in thought from point to point in endless succession and observe no change, and speak in the language of time of that which is thus unalterably abiding as 'eternal.' But it is evident that we cannot apply this 'phantom of succession' to the existence of GOD. The 'eternal' does not in essence express the infinite extension of time but the absence of time: not the omni-temporal but the supra-temporal.

When therefore we declare our belief in 'the life eternal' our meaning is best defined by contrast with the present life. Eternal life is emphatically, as it is described in the corresponding clause of the 'Nicene' Creed, 'the life of the world to come,' the life of 'that age' in opposition to the life of 'this age.' Here conflict and decay are the conditions not only of being but even of happiness. Obstacles and difficulties call out our powers into vigorous activity. But we cannot rest in the prospect of a never-ending conflict. We are forced to regard such broken struggles as transitory. That which is transitory in detail is transitory in the sum. And here our Creed
Heb. ii. 8, 9. meets us. Though *we see not yet all things subject* to the Son of man, we do see in His exaltation the sure pledge of a realised victory. We
1 Cor. xiii. 10. know therefore that *that which is in part shall be*

done away, while we admit that here we can only XI.
think and know 'in part:' we know that in the world and in ourselves shall be revealed the fulness of Christ's redemption and of God's will: we know that there shall be the life which is truly life, the life eternal, the life which is the vision of God, which is (they are amazing words) God John xvii. 3.
made known in His Son.

In two passages of Holy Scripture we have a description of 'the life eternal.' To hold these firmly is to be saved from many perplexities which accompany all attempts to define further that which we have no power to define. *This is the life eternal, that they should know Thee the only true God, and Him Whom Thou didst send, even Jesus Christ.*

We know that the Son of God is come, and hath given us an understanding, that we know Him that is true, and we are in Him that is true, even in His Son Jesus Christ. This is the true God, and eternal life.

Eternal life is then that knowledge of God which is communion with Him: it is not something future but absolute: it *is* in its realisation: it answers to a divine fellowship which issues in perfect unity.

Each of these thoughts may be followed out a little further, though we must keep the most

XI. reverent reserve lest we should seem to determine by conclusions due to the limitations of our own minds what Scripture has not determined.

The eternal life is not something future: it *is*, it is now. It lies in a relation to GOD through Christ. The manifestation of the life is confined and veiled by the circumstances of our present condition, but the life is actual. It does not depend for its essence upon any external
Gal. iv. 9. change. To know GOD, or, as St Paul prefers to express the truth, to be known by GOD, to be the object, in human language, of His thought, is to have entered, to have been taken into the new order. Time has no more connexion with this form of existence in itself than with the being of GOD.

But, while this is so, the teaching of Scripture under the forms of time guards us from supposing that this eternal life, this life in GOD, is a monotonous stillness, a calm, fixed attainment, an extinction of individual consciousness, a Nirvâna. We may not indeed carry into it directly anything which measures and characterises the present, the temporal life; but all these personal feelings, memories, aspirations, fruitions, are a figure of spiritual realities, of the unseen and the unimaginable which shall be. As we are now, the knowledge which is eternal life is spoken of as something continuous, progressive, depending upon effort, springing out of fellowship and issuing in closer fellowship. But the end is fellowship and not absorption. We are said to be 'in Christ;' and we are said also 'to be at home with Christ.' The life is in the growing knowledge. 'To enter into life' suggests the enjoyment of the fulness of powers which are checked and undeveloped here. XI.

Yet once again the eternal life which is fellowship with GOD is presented to us also as fellowship with men, fellowship with men in GOD. The fellowship with GOD, while it is itself the essence of life leaves the personality of the believer unimpaired: so too the fellowship with men, though it appears to be the supreme manifestation of human life in its completeness, leaves the individual life in its entirety, or perhaps we may say more truly first confirms to it its entirety. On such a subject our weakness counsels us to speak with the utmost caution; but may we not say that this idea of a corporate life 'in Christ,' to which each separate life is a conscious contributory, removes many of the gravest difficulties which attend every endeavour to realise the future as an existence of isolated individualities?

There can be no doubt that the uniform tendency of recent research is to establish in many

XI. unexpected ways the closeness of the connexion by which we are bound one to another. In proportion as we know more fully, this connexion is found to be more powerful and more far-reaching. It is the element—one element—in the idea of life which has been specially revealed to us in this age. We may conclude therefore that it is designed by the Providence of GOD for our special use. And it is distinctly recognised in the New Testament. We can now perceive at length that the phrases which describe the dependence of man upon man, and the mutual relations of man and nature, and the divine purpose of uniting all things 'in Christ,' are to be taken literally. They shew us that the divine revelation of life is the revelation of that larger life which we can painfully and dimly see to be now. We have in them the promise, the prophecy, of a life in which there is the unity of infinite peace and the energy of infinite love, the peace of GOD and the love of GOD, 'we in Him and He in us.'

The eternal life has been spoken of as fellow-
2 Pet. i. 4. ship with GOD, 'a participation in the divine nature.' This phrase of St Peter throws light upon the idea which I wish to bring out. We are taught that 'GOD is love,' in His own Being; and the declaration helps us to understand in some way how perfect unity is harmonised with

the interaction of different Persons. We are XI.
taught also that 'love never faileth.' Here then we have an image of that future consummation to which we reach forward. The life which is the expression of love is a life of the whole fulfilled in the life of the parts; a life in which every part enjoys the life of the whole.

We declare our belief in 'the life eternal'—that is faith's proclamation of the fulness of the divine victory—and we go no further. Yet we cannot wholly suppress the questions which arise when we pronounce words full of the largest hope. Does this life exclude death wholly and in all its
forms? Does it include that 'restitution of all Acts iii. 21.
things' which is proposed as the aim of human repentance and effort? Or does it leave room for existences finally alien from GOD and unsubdued by His love, for evil, as evil, enduring as GOD *is*? To suggest this last alternative seems to be to admit the possibility of a dualism in a form wholly inconceivable The present existence of evil carries with it difficulties to which nature offers no solution; but to suppose that evil once introduced into the world is for ever, appears to be at variance with the essential conception of GOD as revealed to us.

There may however be some fallacy in our way of conceiving and stating these questions. We

XI. know too little of the purifying and consuming fire of God's love, too little of the effect of punishment when it is seen in the spiritual completeness of perfect justice, too little of our corporate union one with another in virtue of our common humanity, to be able to form theories as to the world to come. And Scripture does not encourage us to enter on such an effort. The reserve of the prophetic and apostolic writings as to the unseen world is as remarkable as the boldness with which uninspired teachers have presumed to deal with it.

But two thoughts bearing upon the future find clear expression in the New Testament. The one is of the consequences of unrepented sin as answering to the sin; the other of a final unity in which God shall be all in all. We read of an *eternal sin*, of *a sin which has no forgiveness in this world nor in the world to come*, of a debt incurred of which the payment to be rigidly exacted exceeds all imaginable resources of the debtor, of *eternal destruction*, of *the worm that dieth not and the fire that is not quenched*. And on the other side we read of the purpose, the good pleasure of God *to sum up all things in Christ*, and *through Him to reconcile all things unto Himself, whether things upon the earth or things in the heavens*, of the bringing to naught of the last enemy death, and the final subjection of all things to God. XI.

Moreover, it must be added, these apparently antithetical statements correspond with two modes of regarding the subject from the side of reason. If we approach it from the side of man, we see that in themselves the consequences of actions appear to be for the doer like the deed, indelible; and also that the finite freedom of the individual appears to include the possibility of final resistance to God. And again if we approach it from the Divine side, it seems to be an inadmissible limitation of the infinite love of God that a human will should for ever refuse to yield to it in complete self-surrender when it is known as love.

If we are called upon to decide which of these two lines of reasoning, which of these two thoughts of Scripture must be held to prevail, we can hardly doubt that that which is the most comprehensive, that which reaches farthest, contains the ruling idea; and that is the idea of a final divine unity. How it will be reached we are wholly unable to say; but we are sure that the manner, which has not been revealed, will be in perfect harmony with the justice of God and the obligations of man's responsibility. More than this we dare not lay down. But that end—'the

XI. end'—rises before us as the strongest motive and the most certain encouragement in all the labours of the life of faith.

Thus it is that the cycle of our Creed is completed. 'From GOD, unto GOD' is the sum of the history which it discloses, wrought out once for all in the human Life of the Son of GOD, and through the Spirit being still wrought out by His power in the world. The more we ponder over the facts which we confess in the fullest light of all the phenomena which it has been given to us to observe, the more surely shall we find that these facts of the Christian Creed cover the area of human life, of action and of thought. They confirm to us a view of the future, which reconciles the contrasts of the present: they reveal to us a view of the present, which, while it intensifies the motives for personal exertion, adds a calming faith in the sovereignty of the Divine Will. They shew us that there is an eternal significance in our daily struggles, failures, attainments, and that there is a goal for all being: they shew us that we are fashioning day by day not ourselves only but the society to which we belong. They take nothing from the value of the individual soul, and yet they disclose a life immeasurably vaster in which 'the many' shall share.

To the last we see little, and we see dimly. XI.
When the vision seems to grow clearer we are forced by our earthly infirmity to bow the head and veil the face before the exceeding glory. But in the Person of the Lord Jesus Christ we can see the Father. That is enough.

Of Him and through Him and unto Him are all things. To Him be glory for ever. Amen.

NOTE I.

The Idea of Religion.

God that made the world and all things therein...made of one every nation of men for to dwell on all the face of the earth...that they should seek God, if haply they might feel after Him and find Him, though He is not far from each one of us; for in Him we live, and move, and have our being.

Acts xvii. 24—27.

THE greatest ideas are those on which we commonly reflect least, and which from their very comprehensiveness it is most difficult to define. Till recent times those who endeavoured to determine the conception of religion drew their conclusions from an examination of some one positive system of religion with which they were familiar. A larger view of the many religions of the world has now led men to seek in the human constitution the general explanation of that principle or instinct which is variously embodied in various races and in various stages of the development of the same race. NOTE I.

An analysis of man's constitution shews that he is capable of knowing, feeling, acting; and that the energies of knowledge, emotion, will, are grouped round three final self-revealed existences which we speak of generally as self, the world, GOD. The powers exist frequently in a most undisciplined form: the existences are frequently apprehended only in a most rudimentary and partial shape. But experience establishes beyond question that man is so made as to

NOTE I. gain in the normal course of life fuller consciousness of his powers and greater command over them, and also to obtain a more distinct view of the existences to which his personal existence is related.

And more than this: in some form or other man strives to bring into harmony the facts which represent for himself, the world, GOD, and that with regard to his whole nature. He seeks peace in himself, peace with the visible powers about him which his senses directly make known, peace with the invisible powers whose existence he is made to infer from what he observes by the laws of his own nature.

In other words, man is born religious; and religion is the endeavour which he makes to bring into harmony the parts of his own being and the various forms of being without him as far as he has realised them in his individual life[1].

[1] In this connexion the derivation of religion (*relligio*) is of interest. From very early times scholars have been divided as to its root. Some have held that it is to be found in *leg-*, to take up, gather, count, observe, and others in *lig-*, to bind. Both derivations are possible, and perfectly justified by corresponding forms. Cicero adopted the former derivation; and Servius the latter. The earlier usage of *relligio* certainly points to the idea of fearful pondering and awe; but none the less with a true instinct as to the fundamental idea of religion, Augustine decided in favour of the derivation from *re-lig-*. His words are striking: Est enim religio vera qua se uni Deo anima, unde se peccato velut abruperat, reconciliatione religat (*De quant. an.* 80; comp. *De vera rel.* 113; *Retract.* I. 13, 9; yet see on the other side *De civ.* X. 4). Compare also Lactantius *Inst.* IV. 28.

We can trace both in the general history of man and in the experience of our own life how the ideas of self and the finite world have been defined little by little. And so it is also with regard to the unseen, to the idea of God. Our personal retrospect shews how our own conceptions have been modified; and in the world at large we see the thoughts which have been present with ourselves shewn on a grander scale; and we meet with other thoughts baser and more startling. But all witness to the same primal truth. NOTE I.

Man's ideas of unseen powers may be cruel and low, the influence of his belief upon his life may be degrading; yet the fact that he does universally look beyond the seen shews that he is constituted to do so: that this element belongs to his nature.

The full conception of religion involves an effort after a complete harmony of being such as has been already indicated; but the simplest and most characteristic element in religion is, no doubt, the endeavour which man makes to establish a fellowship with some unseen being which has influence over his life.

Even the rudest demon-worship contains the germ of this feeling by which the worshipper seeks to be at one with some power which is adverse to him. It is a witness to something in man by which he is essentially constituted to feel after a fellowship with the unseen no less than with the seen. Fear or love may call out the special manifestations of the feeling,

NOTE I. but they do not account for its existence. And there is no clear evidence that any tribes are destitute of religion in this widest sense.

So far all history, all national and personal experience, confirms the words of Augustine: Thou ...O Lord...hast made us for Thee; and our heart is in unrest till it find rest in Thee.

Tu...Domine...fecisti nos ad Te, et inquietum est cor nostrum donec requiescat in Te (*Conf.* I. 1).

It follows from what has been said that every religion will in some degree aim at supplying knowledge, satisfying feeling, disciplining will: it will, in the judgment of those who hold it, tend to bring harmony to the believer in himself and with his environment and with his destiny. A perfect religion will meet these conditions absolutely under all circumstances.

This is not the place to shew in detail how the historic facts which the Christian Creed embodies and interprets, the Incarnation and Resurrection of the Lord, give all that we require in each region of life, dealing completely with the three fundamental antitheses of our being, that of the seen and unseen (cosmical), that of the finite and infinite (metaphysical), that of man and God (personal).

It may happen that now one element and now another becomes dominant. Christianity appears as a system of dogmatism, or of mysticism, or of moralism, according as the influence of thought or feeling or will unduly prevails. But no one element can be admitted to have a supreme power in that which answers completely to the fulness of life. NOTE I.

These general thoughts admit of being placed in another light. Religion, and Christianity as the absolute religion, deals with 'the true,' 'the good' and 'the beautiful,' the subjects of Philosophy and Ethics and Art, and brings to each subject, which in itself is relative and finite, an element of infinitude, in 'the holy,' a consecration to GOD.

How far then, we may ask, does the New Testament throw light upon this general idea of religion? What elements does it recognise in it? What does it set forward as its aim? On what does it shew that it rests?

1. Man, St Paul says, was made to know GOD:

The GOD that made the world and all things therein, he, being Lord of heaven and earth, dwelleth not in temples made with hands; neither is he served by men's hands, as though he needed any thing, seeing he himself giveth to all life, and breath, and all things; and he made of one every nation of men for to dwell on all the face of the earth, having determined their appointed seasons, and the bounds of their habitation; that they should seek GOD, if haply they might feel after him, and find him, though he is not far from each one of us: for in him we live, and move, and have our being; as certain even of your own poets have said, For we are also his offspring. Acts xvii. 24—28.

NOTE I. Here the object of man's existence, conditioned in each case by local and temporal circumstances, ordained of GOD, is set forth as the continuous search for GOD (ζητεῖν τὸν θεόν), which answers to the description of eternal life as the progressive knowledge of GOD. And the use of the word *feel after*, (ψηλαφήσειαν), seems to point to that direct knowledge answering to the fulness of our present life which the
1 John i. 1. Incarnation supplied.

Compare Acts xiv. 17. Elsewhere St Paul indicates both the power and the failure of man:

Rom. i. 18—25. *For the wrath of GOD is revealed from heaven against all ungodliness and unrighteousness of men, who hold down the truth in unrighteousness; because that which may be known of GOD is manifest in them; for GOD manifested it unto them. For the invisible things of him since the creation of the world are clearly seen, being perceived through the things that are made, even his everlasting power and divinity; that they may be without excuse: because that, knowing GOD, they glorified him not as GOD, neither gave thanks; but became vain in their reasonings, and their senseless heart was darkened. Professing themselves to be wise, they became fools, and changed the glory of the incorruptible GOD for the likeness of an image of corruptible man, and of birds, and fourfooted beasts, and creeping things.*

Wherefore GOD gave them up in the lusts of their hearts unto uncleanness, that their bodies should be dishonoured among themselves: for that they exchanged the truth of GOD for a lie, and worshipped and served the creature rather than the Creator, who is blessed for ever. Amen. NOTE I.

For when Gentiles which have no law do by nature the things of the law, these, having no law, are a law unto themselves: in that they shew the work of the law written in their hearts, their conscience bearing witness therewith, and their thoughts one with another accusing or else excusing them; in the day when GOD shall judge the secrets of men, according to my gospel, by Jesus Christ. Rom. ii. 14—16.

In these passages it is important to consider carefully the extent of man's possible knowledge in the way of nature, *GOD'S everlasting power and divinity*, *the work of the law* (ἥ τε ἀΐδιος αὐτοῦ δύναμις καὶ θειότης, τὸ ἔργον τοῦ νόμου): the seat of his corruption and obedience, *the heart* (ἐσκοτίσθη ἡ ἀσύνετος καρδία, γραπτὸν ἐν ταῖς καρδίαις): the practical consequences of false belief.

2. Each element in Religion—Knowledge, Feeling, Will—finds complete and instructive recognition:

(*a*) *Knowledge.*

The knowledge of divine things is described commonly by two words γνῶσις and ἐπίγνωσις, which both express an active, living, perception of truth, while the latter implies a perception which pierces to the very heart of things.

NOTE I. For the force of ἐπίγνωσις the student will do well to consider the following passages: Rom. i. 28, 32; iii. 20; x. 2; Phil. i. 9; Eph. i. 17 f.; iv. 13; Col. i. 10; ii. 2; iii. 10; 1 Tim. ii. 4; 2 Tim. ii. 25; Tit. i. 1.

'Knowledge' and 'wisdom' are combined: 1 Cor. xii. 8; Rom. xi. 33; Col. ii. 3.

Christian knowledge, which is the essence of life, is necessarily progressive: John xvii. 3 (ἵνα γινώσκωσιν); 1 John v. 20 (and notes). Under this aspect Christianity is 'the Truth,' even as Christ is the Truth. Compare *Introd. to Gospel of St John*, pp. xliv ff.

(*b*) *Feeling.*

In the Gospel 'knowledge' is placed in close connexion with 'love.' In divine things—may we not say, with necessary modifications, in all things?—love is the condition of knowledge. Compare 1 Cor. viii. 2 f.; Gal. iv. 9; Phil. i. 9; 1 John iv. 7 f.; John x. 27; 14 f.

Such love includes devout reverence (εὐσέβεια), which, answering to *pietas* in the widest sense, sees 'God in all things and all things in God' (comp. 1 Tim. iii. 16; Acts iii. 12); and especially a reverence for God Himself (θεοσέβεια, 1 Tim. ii. 10; John ix. 31), which takes the form of godly fear (εὐλάβεια, Heb. v. 7; xii. 28).

(*c*) *Will.*

The exercise of will finds a twofold sphere. Inwardly it is shewn in Faith: outwardly it is shewn in Confession. Compare Rom. x. 8 ff.; 2 Cor. ix. 13; Heb. iii. 1; iv. 14; x. 23; 1 John ii. 23; iv. 2 f. NOTE I.

3. Religion, which thus calls into play the fulness of man's powers, finds an outward expression; and this in three ways.

(*a*) In special acts, observances (θρησκεία): James i. 27; Col. ii. 18; Acts xxvi. 5. Comp. Wisd. xi. 16; xiv. 16, 18, 27.

(*b*) In personal divine service (λατρεία, 'servitus relligionis quam λατρεύειν Graeci vocant,' Aug. *de Civ.* v. 15), which expresses specially willing surrender, self-sacrifice. Compare Rom. xii. 1; Apoc. xxii. 3; John xvi. 2.

In the LXX. the word is always used of service of God (or gods).

(*c*) In public official representative service (λειτουργία): Acts xiii. 2. Comp. Rom. xv. 16; Phil. ii. 17.

The word is commonly used in the LXX. of the Jewish priestly service (Hebr. x. 11; Luke i. 23; comp. Hebr. viii. 6); but not exclusively of sacred service (as λατρεύειν). Compare Rom. xiii. 6; xv. 27; 2 Cor. x. 12; Phil. ii. 25, 30.

In connexion with the outward practical aspect of religion, Christ is spoken of as 'the Way:' Acts ix. 2; xix. 9, 23; xxiv. 22. True belief is inseparable from right action: 1 John iv. 8, 20, 21.

4. The end of the Revelation of Christ and of

NOTE I. the Religion which rests upon it is the realisation of that perfect harmony in finite being which answers to the counsel of Creation. This harmony is regarded both in respect of man and of the world:

(*a*) Man.

John xvii. 20 f. *Neither for these only do I pray, but for them also that believe on me through their word; that they may all be one; even as thou, Father, art in me, and I in thee, that they also may be in us: that the world may believe that thou didst send me.*

1 John i. 3, 4. *That which we have seen and heard declare we unto you also, that ye also may have fellowship with us: yea, and our fellowship is with the Father, and with his Son Jesus Christ: and these things we write, that our joy may be fulfilled.*

Gal. iii. 27 f. *For as many of you as were baptized into Christ did put on Christ. There can be neither Jew nor Greek, there can be neither bond nor free, there can be no male and female: for ye all are one man in Christ Jesus.*

1 Thess. v. 23. *And the* GOD *of peace himself sanctify you wholly; and may your spirit and soul and body be preserved entire, without blame at the coming of our Lord Jesus Christ.*

Eph. ii. 14—18. *For he is our peace, who made both one, and brake down the middle wall of partition, having abolished in his flesh the enmity, even the law of commandments contained in ordinances; that he might create in him-*

self of the twain one new man, so making peace; and NOTE I.
might reconcile them both in one body unto GOD through the cross, having slain the enmity thereby: and he came and preached peace to you that were far off, and peace to them that were nigh: for through him we both have our access in one Spirit unto the Father.

(*b*) Finite being generally.

The earnest expectation of the creation waiteth for Rom. viii. 19—23.
the revealing of the sons of GOD. For the creation was subjected to vanity, not of its own will, but by reason of him who subjected it, in hope that the creation itself also shall be delivered from the bondage of corruption into the liberty of the glory of the children of GOD. For we know that the whole creation groaneth and travaileth in pain together until now. And not only so, but ourselves also, which have the firstfruits of the Spirit, even we ourselves groan within ourselves, waiting for our adoption, to wit, the redemption of our body.

The last enemy that shall be abolished is death. 1 Cor. xv. 26—28.
For, He put all things in subjection under his feet. But when he saith, All things are put in subjection, it is evident that he is excepted who did subject all things unto him. And when all things have been subjected unto him, then shall the Son also himself be subjected to him that did subject all things unto him, that GOD may be all in all.

[*In the Beloved*] *we have our redemption through* Eph. i. 7—10.

NOTE I. *his blood, the forgiveness of our trespasses, according to the riches of his grace, which he made to abound toward us in all wisdom and prudence, having made known unto us the mystery of his will, according to his good pleasure which he purposed in him unto a dispensation of the fulness of the times, to sum up all things in Christ, the things in the heavens, and the things upon the earth.*

Col. i. 19, 20. *For it was the good pleasure of the Father that in him should all the fulness dwell; and through him to reconcile all things unto himself, having made peace through the blood of his cross; through him, I say, whether things upon the earth, or things in the heavens.*

5. The whole revelation in its source and in its power comes from the grace of Him Who is Love. It rests upon an Ordering, a Disposition, of GOD (διαθήκη), and not upon a Covenant (συνθήκη), where man can discuss the terms which he accepts though usage has made Covenant the Biblical representative of the former term.

Heb. viii. 7—13. (Jer. xxxi. 31—34.) *For if that first covenant had been faultless, then would no place have been sought for a second. For finding fault with them, he saith,*

> *Behold, the days come, saith the Lord,*
> *That I will make a new covenant with the house of Israel and with the house of Judah;*
> *Not according to the covenant that I made with their fathers*

In the day that I took them by the hand to lead them forth out of the land of Egypt; NOTE I.
For they continued not in my covenant,
And I regarded them not, saith the Lord.
For this is the covenant that I will make with the house of Israel
After those days, saith the Lord;
I will put my laws into their mind,
And on their heart also will I write them:
And I will be to them a GOD,
And they shall be to me a people:
And they shall not teach every man his fellow-citizen,
And every man his brother, saying, Know the Lord:
For all shall know me,
From the least to the greatest of them.
For I will be merciful to their iniquities,
And their sins will I remember no more.

In that he saith, A new covenant, he hath made the first old. But that which is becoming old and waxeth aged is nigh unto vanishing away.

NOTE II.

The Idea of Faith.

We walk by faith, not by sight.

2 Cor. v. 7.

Faith is the substance of things hoped for, the test of things not seen.

Hebr. xi. 1.

ALL action involves an advance into the unseen, and we are so constituted as necessarily to act. We believe in the general permanence of observed laws; we believe in the general permanence of the character of friends; and act without hesitation on our belief. Such belief is wholly different from a belief in past facts which rests on testimony. NOTE II.

We may here leave out of further consideration the nature of our belief in the permanence of natural 'laws,' represented in its simplest form by the first 'law of motion.' This belief, though it prepares the way for our belief in the general permanence of human character is yet different from it in kind. The one deals essentially with fixed conditions, the other with variable conditions due to a vital progress.

Faith properly belongs to the latter, to the relations of life. It is the basis of all personal dealings of man with man; and also of man with any other being whom he apprehends personally. It is evident beyond question that man is so constituted as to have Faith which makes social life possible. By Faith he enters confidently on the future and the unseen: without it the future and the unseen world have for

NOTE II. him no reality. The opposite to Faith is not Reason but Sight.

The highest form of Faith is religious Faith, by which we acknowledge that there is a divine purpose of wisdom and love being wrought out in the world, and that we are called upon and enabled to cooperate towards its fulfilment. This purpose, partially seen in creation and life and dimly shadowed out under the Old Covenant, has been fully disclosed in the Incarnation (Rom. xvi. 25 ff.). The consideration of such a purpose involves the recognition of One Whose will it expresses. We fashion a human conception of His character from all that we can learn of His working. And just as we read in the past the character of a friend or of a parent, and without doubt trust ourselves to our interpretation of it for the future, so it is with our interpretation of the facts through which GOD has been pleased to make Himself known. We interpret them more or less perfectly and throw ourselves upon the conclusions which we have drawn with practical assurance.

This assurance is not due solely to an intellectual process, nor to feeling, nor to will. Knowledge, emotion, volition all contribute to the result. The Faith, on which it rests, is a harmonious energy of man's whole nature. It corresponds with religion which is its proper object. Man, as we have seen, is born for religion, and he is born for faith through which he realises the characteristic facts of religion.

Thus Faith includes three elements: NOTE II.

1. A conviction of the truth of that to which it is directed.

2. A quickening of love by which the conviction is made personal confidence.

3. A readiness for action corresponding to the conviction.

The starting-point in the establishment of Faith is knowledge. Certain facts are apprehended clearly which point to certain conclusions in regard to the future and the unseen. We are so made as to draw these conclusions. Such conclusions are not distinguished from conclusions as to past facts resting on testimony as more or less certain in the same line. We may be equally certain that the battle of Waterloo was fought at a particular time and place, that the sun will rise to-morrow, and that a parent will love his child, but the certainty is reached by different ways, and no comparison can be made between the degrees of cogency belonging to the several forms of evidence on which they rest.

The facts which call out Faith in the ordinary conduct of life suggest the presence of a greater counsel of love wrought out in the visible order. This, when it is once grasped, we necessarily refer to a 'Person,' to God; and as we recognise it we learn to trust Him. The conviction, which was based on knowledge, is now inspired by feeling; and it is in

NOTE II. this passage from an intellectual conclusion to the sense of a personal relation in regard to the unseen that we can recognise the working of the divine element without which Faith cannot be.

But we cannot rest in feeling only. The will which we recognise is to be fulfilled, and we have a part in the fulfilment.

It often happens, as in the case of Religion, that the name 'Faith' is applied to a frame of mind in which one or more of its constituent elements is wholly absent or imperfectly represented. Sometimes an intellectual conviction, sometimes a determination of will is called faith. Sometimes the emotional element overpowers the other two. But in each case the incompleteness of the energy in relation to the whole man is evident.

Faith is indeed the energy of our whole nature directed to the highest form of being. Faith gives stability to our view of the universe. As soon as we pass outside ourselves, beyond deductions from the limitations of our own minds, we rest on Faith. By Faith we are convinced that our impressions of things without are not dreams or delusions, but for us true representations of our environment. By Faith we are convinced that the signs of permanence, order, progress, which we observe in nature are trustworthy. By Faith we are convinced that fellowship is possible with our fellow-men and with God.

The general conception of Faith which has been

thus outlined is fully confirmed by the teaching of the New Testament. It will be sufficient to indicate some lines of inquiry which can be followed out in detailed study. NOTE II.

1. The sphere of Faith.

Faith is the substance of things hoped for, the test of things not seen. Hebr. xi. 1.

By faith he forsook Egypt...for he endured as seeing Him Who is invisible. Id. v. 27.

We walk by faith, not by sight (comp. c. iv. 18). 2 Cor. v. 7.

Whom [Jesus Christ] not having seen ye love; on whom, though now ye see Him not, yet believing, ye rejoice greatly with joy unspeakable and full of glory. 1 Pet. i. 8.

Without entering upon disputed details of interpretation it is clear that the sphere of faith as described in these passages is the future and the unseen; or in other words that which cannot be directly witnessed by testimony, or apprehended by the senses. Faith brings conviction in regard to truths not otherwise capable of being determined.

2. The special object of Faith.

The special object of Faith is a Divine Name, that is a Divine Person made known to men and recognised by them. By Faith man enters into fellowship with God in Christ.

As many as received Him [the Word] to them gave John i. 12.

NOTE II. *He the right to become children of GOD, even to them that believed on His name.*

Acts iii. 16. *By faith in His name hath His name made this man strong, whom ye behold and know; yea, the faith which is through Him hath given him this perfect soundness in the presence of you all.*

1 John v. 13. *These things have I written unto you, that ye may know that ye have eternal life, even unto you that believe on the name of the Son of GOD.*

John xx. 31. *These [things] are written that ye may believe that Jesus is the Christ, the Son of GOD; and that believing ye may have life in His name.*

With this fulness of faith on a Divine Person (πιστεύειν εἰς) must be compared the different partial activities of faith. He who believes in the revealed Person believes the whole revelation about Him (πιστεύειν τῷ ὀνόματι, 1 John. iii 23, note), and definite points in that revelation to be true (πιστεύειν ὅτι, 1 John v. 1, 5); and also believes Him (πιστεύετέ μοι, John xiv. 11).

The passage Acts iii. 16 is singularly instructive as representing in combination the divine principle in faith (ἡ πίστις ἡ δι' αὐτοῦ), the human activity in faith (τῇ πίστει τοῦ ὀνόματος αὐτοῦ), the energy of the object of faith (ἐστερέωσε τὸ ὄνομα αὐτοῦ).

3. The elements of Faith.

Faith, it has been seen, includes elements of knowledge, feeling, action.

(*a*) Knowledge. NOTE II.

Faith cometh of hearing. Rom. x. 17.

Comp. Luke viii. 12; John i. 7; 1 Cor. iii. 5 ff. The right interpretation of the past leads to the understanding of the present: John v. 46.

(*b*) Feeling.

The knowledge of 'the Name of Christ,' of the revelation, that is, of the Father and of the Son, involves and issues in love.

Beloved, let us love one another: for love is of GOD; and every one that loveth is begotten of GOD, and knoweth GOD. He that loveth not knoweth not GOD; for GOD is love. 1 John iv. 7 f.

(*c*) Action.

Love must if it be real prove itself in action.

Hereby know we love, because he laid down his life for us: and we ought to lay down our lives for the brethren. But whoso hath the world's goods, and beholdeth his brother in need, and shutteth up his compassion from him, how doth the love of GOD abide in him? 1 John iii. 16 f.

If a man say, I love GOD, and hateth his brother, he is a liar: for he that loveth not his brother whom he hath seen, cannot love GOD whom he hath not seen. 1 John iv. 20.

4. The seat of Faith.

The seat of faith is 'the heart,' the seat of individual character and of moral determination.

NOTE II. Rom. x. 10. *With the heart man believeth unto righteousness; and with the mouth confession is made unto salvation.*

5. The activity of Faith.

The various aspects of the effect of faith is shewn in 'life,' 'righteousness,' 'salvation,' 'power.'

(*a*) Life.

Consider John iii. 36; 1 Tim. i. 16; John xi. 25 f.

(*b*) Righteousness.

In this case it is necessary to distinguish the different relations in which righteousness is placed to faith. It comes 'by faith' (πίστει) as the instrument (Rom. iii. 28); 'of faith' (ἐκ πίστεως) as the source (Gal. ii. 16; iii. 8, 24; Rom. v. 1; ix. 30; x. 6); 'through faith' (διὰ πίστεως) as the effective power (Gal. iii. 9; Rom. iii. 22, (30)). Faith also characterises the righteousness (δικ. πίστεως, Rom. iv. 13, 11).

Compare Hebr. xi. 3 (πίστει), 13 (κατὰ πίστιν), 33 (διὰ πίστεως).

(*c*) Salvation.

Under this head the use of the phrase 'thy faith hath saved thee' requires to be carefully considered:

Matt. ix. 22 ‖ Mk. v. 34 ‖ Lk. viii. 48.

Mk. x. 52 ‖ Lk. xviii. 42.

Luke vii. 50.

—— xvii. 19.

There is a unity in man's whole nature which must be recognised.

Compare Acts iii. 16; xiv. 9; and Gal. iii. 14, 22, 26. NOTE II.

Without Faith man is in darkness (John xii. 46; Heb. xi. 6), falsehood (1 John ii. 22 f.; iii. 14), death (John iii. 18, 36; viii. 24).

Generally Faith is the condition of the Divine working (Mk. v. 36 *only believe* πίστευε ‖ Lk. viii. 50 πίστευσον; Mk. ix. 23 f. *if thou canst*...; and negatively, Matt. xiii. 58 ‖ Mk. vi. 5 f. *he could not*; Matt. xvii. 19 f.); and the measure of the Divine gift (Matt. viii. 13; ix. 29; xxi. 22 ‖ Mk. xi. 23 f.). The power of Faith is unlimited (Matt. xxi. 21; Mk. ix. 23).

The obstacles to Faith are clearly marked: John v. 44; xii. 39 ff.; 43.

One further remark must be added. Faith belongs to the life of man as he was created, in his essential nature. For man fallen the necessary supplement of Faith is Repentance, which like Faith includes elements of knowledge, feeling, will.

NOTE III.

The Creeds.

With the heart man believeth unto righteousness; and with the mouth confession is made unto salvation.

ROM. x. 10.

Hold the pattern of sound words.

2 TIM. i. 13.

The original texts of the Nicene and Constantinopolitan Creeds, together with the earliest and the received Latin Versions of the latter Creed, given in the following pages, will repay careful study.

I have added also the earliest Greek and Latin texts of the Roman Creed for comparison with the complete form of the Creed which gained general currency in the West after the eighth century.

CREED OF NICÆA[1].

πιστεύομεν
εἰς ἕνα θεὸν πατέρα παντοκράτορα

πάντων ὁρατῶν τε καὶ ἀοράτων ποιητήν
καὶ εἰς ἕνα κύριον Ἰησοῦν Χριστόν
τὸν υἱὸν τοῦ θεοῦ
γεννηθέντα ἐκ τοῦ πατρὸς μονογενῆ

τοῦτ' ἐστὶν ἐκ τῆς οὐσίας τοῦ πατρός
θεὸν ἐκ θεοῦ
φῶς ἐκ φωτός
θεὸν ἀληθινὸν ἐκ θεοῦ ἀληθινοῦ
γεννηθέντα οὐ ποιηθέντα
ὁμοούσιον τῷ πατρί
δι' οὗ τὰ πάντα ἐγένετο
τά τε ἐν τῷ οὐρανῷ καὶ τὰ ἐν τῇ γῇ
τὸν δι' ἡμᾶς τοὺς ἀνθρώπους καὶ διὰ τὴν ἡμετέραν σωτηρίαν
κατελθόντα
καὶ σαρκωθέντα

CREED OF CONSTANTINOPLE[2].

πιστεύομεν
εἰς ἕνα θεὸν πατέρα παντοκράτορα
ποιητὴν οὐρανοῦ καὶ γῆς
ὁρατῶν τε πάντων καὶ ἀοράτων
καὶ εἰς ἕνα κύριον Ἰησοῦν Χριστόν
τὸν υἱὸν τοῦ θεοῦ
τὸν μονογενῆ τὸν ἐκ τοῦ πατρὸς γεννηθέντα
πρὸ πάντων τῶν αἰώνων

φῶς ἐκ φωτός
θεὸν ἀληθινὸν ἐκ θεοῦ ἀληθινοῦ
γεννηθέντα οὐ ποιηθέντα
ὁμοούσιον τῷ πατρί
δι' οὗ τὰ πάντα ἐγένετο

τὸν δι' ἡμᾶς τοὺς ἀνθρώπους καὶ διὰ τὴν ἡμετέραν σωτηρίαν
κατελθόντα ἐκ τῶν οὐρανῶν
καὶ σαρκωθέντα ἐκ πνεύματος ἁγίου καὶ Μαρίας τῆς παρθένου

ἐνανθρωπήσαντα	καὶ ἐνανθρωπήσαντα
	σταυρωθέντα τε ὑπὲρ ἡμῶν ἐπὶ Ποντίου Πιλάτου
παθόντα	καὶ παθόντα
	καὶ ταφέντα
καὶ ἀναστάντα τῃ τρίτῃ ἡμέρᾳ	καὶ ἀναστάντα τῇ τρίτῃ ἡμέρᾳ κατὰ τὰς γραφάς
ἀνελθόντα εἰς τοὺς οὐρανούς	καὶ ἀνελθόντα εἰς τοὺς οὐρανούς
	καὶ καθεζόμενον ἐκ δεξιῶν τοῦ πατρός
καὶ ἐρχόμενον κρῖναι ζῶντας καὶ νεκρούς	καὶ πάλιν ἐρχόμενον μετὰ δόξης κρῖναι ζῶντας καὶ νεκρούς
	οὗ τῆς βασιλείας οὐκ ἔσται τέλος
καὶ εἰς τὸ ἅγιον πνεῦμα	καὶ εἰς τὸ πνεῦμα τὸ ἅγιον
	τὸ κύριον τὸ ζωοποιόν
	τὸ ἐκ τοῦ πατρὸς ἐκπορευόμενον
	τὸ σὺν πατρὶ καὶ υἱῷ συμπροσκυνούμενον καὶ συνδοξαζόμενον
	τὸ λαλῆσαν διὰ τῶν προφητῶν
	εἰς μίαν ἁγίαν καθολικὴν καὶ ἀποστολικὴν ἐκκλησίαν
	ὁμολογοῦμεν ἓν βάπτισμα
	εἰς ἄφεσιν ἁμαρτιῶν
	προσδοκῶμεν ἀνάστασιν νεκρῶν
	καὶ ζωὴν τοῦ μέλλοντος αἰῶνος
τοὺς δὲ λέγοντας ἦν ποτε ὅτε οὐκ ἦν καὶ πρὶν γεννηθῆναι οὐκ ἦν καὶ ὅτι ἐξ οὐκ ὄντων ἐγένετο ἢ ἐξ ἑτέρας ὑποστάσεως ἢ οὐσίας φάσκοντας εἶναι ἢ κτιστὸν ἢ τρεπτὸν ἢ ἀλλοιωτὸν τὸν υἱὸν τοῦ θεοῦ ἀναθεματίζει ἡ καθολικὴ ἐκκλησία.	Ἀμήν.

[1] Hahn, *Bibliothek der Symbole*... § 73.

[2] Hahn, *a. a. O.* § 75.

Latin Version of the 'Constantinopolitan' Creed by Dionysius Exiguus (c. A.D. 500)[1].	Latin Version of the 'Constantinopolitan' Creed included in the Acts of the Third Council of Toledo, A.D. 589 (Labbe ed. Coleti, vi. 697).	The 'Nicene' Creed as ratified by the Council of Trent, Sess. iii. A.D. 1546.
Credimus	Credimus	Credo
in unum Deum Patrem omnipotentem	*in unum Deum Patrem omnipotentem*	*in unum Deum Patrem omnipotentem*
factorem cæli et terræ	*factorem cæli et terræ*	*factorem cæli et terræ*
visibilium omnium et invisibilium	*visibilium omnium et invisibilium* conditorem	*visibilium omnium et invisibilium*
Et in unum Dominum Jesum Christum	*Et in unum Dominum Jesum Christum*	*Et in unum Dominum Jesum Christum*
Filium Dei	*Filium Dei* unigenitum	*Filium Dei* unigenitum
natum ex Patre ante omnia sæcula	*ex Patre natum ante omnia sæcula*	et *ex Patre natum ante omnia sæcula*
	Deum ex Deo	Deum de Deo
	Lumen ex Lumine	Lumen de Lumine
Deum verum de *Deo vero*	*Deum verum* ex *Deo vero*	*Deum verum* de *Deo vero*
natum *non factum*	Natum *non factum*	Genitum *non factum*
consubstantialem *Patri*	homoousion *Patri*	consubstantialem *Patri*
	hoc est, eiusdem substantiæ cum Patre	
per quem omnia facta sunt	*per quem omnia facta sunt*	*per quem omnia facta sunt*
	quæ iu cælo et quæ in terra	
qui propter nos homines	*qui propter nos*	*qui propter nos* homines
et salutem nostram	*et* propter *nostram salutem*	*et* propter *nostram salutem*
descendit de cælis	*descendit*	*descendit* de cælis
et incarnatus est	*et incarnatus est*	*et incarnatus est*

de Spiritu Sancto ex Maria Virgine	*de Spiritu Sancto ex Maria Virgine*	*de Spiritu Sancto ex Maria Virgine*
et humanatus est	homo factus	et homo factus est
et crucifixus est pro nobis		crucifixus etiam pro nobis
sub Pontio *Pilato*	passus est *sub Pilato*	*sub* Pontio *Pilato* passus
et *sepultus* est	*sepultus*	et *sepultus* est
et *resurrexit tertia die*	*tertia die resurrexit*	Et *resurrexit tertia die*
		secundum Scripturas
adscendit in cælum	*adscendit in* cælos	et *adscendit in* cælum
sedet ad dexteram Patris	*sedet ad dexteram Patris*	*sedet ad dexteram Patris*
iterum venturus cum *gloria*	*iterum venturus* in *gloria*	et *iterum venturus* est cum *gloria*
iudicare vivos et mortuos	*iudicare vivos et mortuos*	*iudicare vivos et mortuos*
cuius regni non erit finis	*cuius regni non erit finis*	*cuius regni non erit finis*
Et	Credimus *et*	*Et*
in Spiritum Sanctum	*in Spiritum Sanctum*	*in Spiritum Sanctum*
Dominum et vivificantem	*Dominum et* vivificatorem	*Dominum et* vivificantem
ex Patre procedentem	*ex Patre* et Filio procedentem	qui *ex Patre* Filioque procedit
cum Patre et Filio	*cum Patre et Filio*	qui *cum Patre et Filio*
adorandum et conglorificandum	adorandum et glorificandum	simul adoratur et conglorificatur
qui locutus est per sanctos *prophetas*	*qui locutus est per Prophetas*	*qui locutus est per Prophetas*
Et *unam* sanctam *catholicam* et *apostolicam Ecclesiam*	*unam catholicam* atque *apostolicam Ecclesiam*	et *unam* sanctam *catholicam* et *apostolicam Ecclesiam*
Confitemur *unum baptisma*	Confitemur *unum baptisma*	Confiteor *unum baptisma*
in remissionem peccatorum	*in remissionem peccatorum*	*in remissionem peccatorum*
expectamus *resurrectionem mortuorum*	expectamus *resurrectionem mortuorum*	et expecto *resurrectionem mortuorum*
et vitam futuri *sæculi*	*et vitam sæculi*	*et vitam* venturi *sæculi*
Amen.	Amen.	Amen.

[1] The received Latin forms of the 'Apostles'' and 'Nicene' Creeds are given with a very convenient summary of various readings by Streitwolf and Klener, *Libri Symbolici Ecclesiæ Catholicæ*, i. pp. 3 ff.

THE ROMAN CREED.

MARCELLUS of Ancyra, c. A.D. 337.	RUFINUS c. A.D. 390.	PIRMINIUS, c. A.D. 750.
πιστεύω	Credo	Credo
εἰς θεὸν * * παντοκράτορα καὶ	in Deum Patrem omnipotentem	in Deum Patrem omnipotentem
* *	* * et	Creatorem cæli et terræ[1]; et
εἰς Χριστὸν Ἰησοῦν τὸν υἱὸν αὐτοῦ	in Christum Jesum unicum	in Jesum Christum, Filium
τὸν μονογενῆ	Filium eius	eius unicum
τὸν κύριον ἡμῶν	Dominum nostrum	Dominum nostrum
τὸν γεννηθέντα ἐκ Πνεύματος Ἁγίου	Qui natus est de Spiritu Sancto	Qui conceptus est de Spiritu Sancto
καὶ * * Μαρίας τῆς Παρθένου	* * ex Maria Virgine	Natus ex Maria Virgine[2]
τὸν ἐπὶ Ποντίου Πιλάτου * *	* * crucifixus	Passus sub Pontio Pilato
σταυρωθέντα	sub Pontio Pilato	Crucifixus
* * καὶ	* * et	Mortuus et
ταφέντα	Sepultus	Sepultus[2]
* * * καὶ	* * *	Descendit ad inferna[3]
τῇ τρίτῃ ἡμέρᾳ ἀναστάντα ἐκ τῶν νεκρῶν	Tertia die resurrexit a mortuis	Tertia die resurrexit a mortuis
ἀναβάντα εἰς τοὺς οὐρανοὺς καὶ	Ascendit in cælos	Ascendit ad cælos
καθήμενον ἐν δεξιᾷ * * τοῦ Πατρὸς * *	Sedet ad dexteram * * Patris * *	Sedit(-et) ad dexteram Dei Patris omnipotentis
ὅθεν ἔρχεται	Inde venturus est	Inde venturus est
κρίνειν ζῶντας καὶ νεκρούς.	Judicare vivos et mortuos;	Judicare vivos et mortuos;
καὶ	et	Credo
εἰς τὸ Ἅγιον Πνεῦμα	in Spiritum Sanctum	in Spiritum Sanctum
ἁγίαν ἐκκλησίαν	Sanctam Ecclesiam	Sanctam Ecclesiam
* *	* *	Catholicam[4]
* *	* *	Sanctorum communionem[5]
ἄφεσιν ἁμαρτιῶν	Remissionem peccatorum	Remissionem peccatorum
σαρκὸς ἀνάστασιν	Carnis resurrectionem.	Carnis resurrectionem
ζωὴν αἰώνιον.		Vitam æternam[6].

[1] A clause corresponding to this is found in the Creeds of Irenæus and Tertullian. It is not found again in a Western Creed till far into the 7th century. [2] The full form of these articles is not found (with one doubtful exception in a sermon attributed to Augustine) till the 7th century. [3] This article is given by Rufinus as part of the Creed of Aquileia in his time. A corresponding article is found in an (Arian) Creed of the Synod of Sirmium A.D. 359 and in two others moulded on it. [4] This epithet is found in the Western Creed in Nicetas A.D. 458 (Hahn, § 25). It is almost universal in Eastern Creeds. [5] This article occurs in the Creed of Faustus of Riez in the second half of the 5th cent., but it was not universal till the end of the 8th cent. [6] This article was not established in the Creed till about the middle of the 7th cent.

THE outline of the Christian Creed is given in the divine institution of Baptism: *Make disciples of all the nations, baptizing them into* NOTE III. Matt. xxviii. 19.

THE NAME OF

THE FATHER, AND

THE SON, AND

THE HOLY GHOST.

For some time it appears that a simple confession corresponding to this description of the divine fellowship to which believers are admitted by incorporation into the Christian Church formed the Baptismal Creed[1].

[1] Traces of the expansion of the first two articles of the Confession are found in 1 Cor. viii. 6, *To us there is*

ONE GOD, THE FATHER,

of whom are all things, and we unto Him; and

ONE LORD, JESUS CHRIST,

through whom are all things, and we through Him.

The simple declaration JESUS IS LORD (1 Cor. xii. 3; Rom. x. 9) contains implicitly the whole Gospel. Comp. Acts xvi. 31. The Confession which is found in the common texts in Acts viii. 37 is an early addition known to Irenæus and Cyprian. The words of the Confession vary in some respects in different authorities.

NOTE III. *Ep.* lxxvi. *ad Magn.* Thus the North African Creed found in CYPRIAN (c. 250) seems to have been

'I believe
in GOD the Father,
in His Son Christ,
in the Holy Ghost.
I believe [the fact of][1]
the remission of sins, and
eternal life
through the Holy Church'.

Catech. xix. § 9. About a century later, in the time of CYRIL (c. 350), a similar form was still in use in the Church of Jerusalem.

'I believe
in the Father, and
in the Son, and
in the Holy Ghost, and
in one Baptism of repentance.'

But it was natural and even necessary that the three fundamental articles, which have received some development in these most elementary Confessions, should be written out at greater length; and not less natural that in the process typical and complementary distinctions in the apprehension of the Faith should become manifest in the East and West.

So it came to pass that in the East, to speak generally, the development of the Baptismal Confession was guided by a dogmatic instinct, and in the

[1] Credo in Deum...credo remissionem peccatorum...

West, by a historic instinct. In the Eastern Creeds, NOTE III. to use a modern form of expression, the 'ideas' of Christianity predominate: in the Western Creeds the 'facts' of Christianity stand out in their absolute simplicity. It is of course obvious that 'idea' and 'fact' in this case correspond completely to two different aspects of the same Truth; but still it is important to observe that both aspects have a distinct recognition in our Catholic formularies, and that the two great ancient divisions of Christendom were providentially fitted to represent them. In the earliest glimpses of the Creed which we can gain the distinction is as yet rudimentary. Traces of Eastern phraseology appear, for example, in the Creeds of Irenæus and Tertullian; but in the fourth century the two types were permanently separated[1].

These types are represented for us in their completest form by the Apostles' Creed, and the 'Nicene' (Constantinopolitan) Creed, as they stand in our Prayer-Book in Morning and Evening Prayer and the Communion Service:

[1] Compare Dr Swete, *The Apostles' Creed: its relation to primitive Christianity.* 1894. A. E. Burn, *An Introduction to the Creeds and to the Te Deum.* 1899.

NOTE III.

The Apostles' Creed[1].

I believe

I. 1. In God the Father Almighty,
Maker of heaven and earth[2]: and

[1] The interrogatory form of the Apostles' Creed in the Services for *Public Baptism of Infants* and *the Visitation of the Sick* offers numerous variations from the form of the Creed in Morning and Evening Prayer:

His *only-begotten* Son,
He *went down* into hell,
did rise again the third day (Eastern order),
at the right hand,
come *again at the end of the world* to judge...
the *Remission* of sins,
the Resurrection of the *flesh*,
everlasting life *after death*.

Other variations occur in the version given in the *Short Catechism* (1553):

He *went up to* heaven,
I believe the holy *universal* church,
the rising again of the flesh.

The Creed is not printed at length in the Morning or Evening Prayer in the Book of 1549 but it is given there in the *Catechism* in the form which was adopted in the Book of 1552 and afterwards.

The addition in the last clause *after death* is found in the short interrogatory Creed in the Salisbury *Manual:* Heurtley, p. 114.

There is an interesting series of English Mediæval versions of the Creed in Wright and Halliwell, *Reliquiæ Antiquæ*, i. p. 38 (xiv cent.); p. 42 (in Kentish dialect, 1340); p. 57 (xiii

THE WESTERN FORM OF THE CONSTANTINOPOLITAN (NICENE) CREED. NOTE III.

I believe[3]

I. 1. In *One* GOD the Father Almighty,
Maker of heaven and earth, *and*
of all things visible and invisible; and

cent.); p. 282 (xiii cent.). To these Maskell (*Monum. Rit.* iii. 251 ff.) adds two more (xiv and xv cent.) and the version of the Primer of 1538.

In the Cambridge MS. Gg. iv. 32 (xiv cent.), from which Halliwell gives a metrical paraphrase of the Creed, there are English and French versions in which the twelve Articles are assigned to the twelve Apostles.

The renderings of the clause *carnis resurrectionem* are worth noting: *uprisigen of fleyes, arysnesse of flesse, fleiss uprising* (xiii cent.), *agenrisyng of fleisch, flessces uprist* (xiv cent.), *risyng of flesshe unto ay lastynge lif* (xv cent.). The epithet *catholicam* is rendered in one MS. only (xiv cent.). The Cambridge text gives 'sothfast holy churche.'

[2] This was the last clause added to the Creed. It does not appear till about 650 A.D.

[3] The original Greek form is *We believe.*

NOTE III. II. 2. In Jesus Christ
His only Son *our Lord*,

Who
3. was *conceived* by the Holy Ghost,
Born of the Virgin Mary,

4. Suffered under Pontius Pilate,

5. was crucified, *dead*, and buried,
He descended into hell[1];
6. The third day he rose again *from the dead*,

[1] This Article appears first in the Aquileian Creed in Rufinus, c. 390 A.D.

II. 2. In *One Lord* Jesus Christ NOTE III.
the only-*begotten* Son *of* GOD[1],
Begotten[2] *of his Father before all worlds,*
GOD of GOD[3],
Light of Light,
Very GOD of very GOD,
Begotten, not made,
Being of one substance with the Father;
By[4] *whom all things were made.*

3. Who *for us men, and for our salvation,*
came down from heaven, and
was *Incarnate* by the Holy Ghost of the Virgin Mary, and
was made man, and

4. was crucified *also for us* under Pontius Pilate.

5. *He* suffered *and was* buried, *and*

6. the third day he rose again[5] *according to the Scripture, and*

[1] Rufinus called attention to the different arrangement of the clauses in this Article in the Western and Eastern Creeds.

[2] The mediæval Latin texts give *et ex Patre natum* (*genitum* below).

[3] This is an addition to the original Constantinopolitan Creed.

[4] The exact rendering is '*through*' (*διά per* not *ὑπό*). So we should read '*through the prophets.*'

[5] The order of the words in this clause differs in the Eastern and Western Creeds. The Greek order is: *he rose again the third day.*

NOTE III.

7. *He* ascended into heaven, and sitteth on the right hand of *GOD* the Father *Almighty;*
8. *From thence* he shall come to judge the quick and the dead.

I believe

III. 9. In the Holy Ghost;

10. *The holy* Catholic Church; *The Communion of Saints*[1];
11. The *Forgiveness* of sins;
12. The Resurrection of the *body*, and the life *everlasting*. Amen.

[1] This Article appears first in the Creed of Faustus of Riez (c. 470).

NOTE III.

7. ascended into heaven, and
sitteth on the right hand of the Father.
And
8. he shall come *again with glory* to judge
both the quick and the dead.
Whose kingdom shall have no end.

And I believe

III. 9. In the Holy Ghost,
The Lord and Giver of life,
Who proceedeth from the Father
and the Son[1].
Who with the Father and the Son together
is worshipped and glorified,
Who spake by the Prophets.
And I believe
10. *One*[2] Catholick *and Apostolick* Church.
I acknowledge
11. *One Baptism* for the *remission* of sins, *and*
I look for
12. the Resurrection of the *dead*, and
the life *of the world to come.* Amen.

[1] This clause 'and the Son' (filioque), which is not found in the Greek text, appears together with the clause 'God of God' in the Latin version of the Creed recited at the third Council of Toledo, 589 A.D.

[2] The epithet *sanctam* is omitted in the Toletan text and in not a few mediæval Latin texts. There is no variation in the Greek.

NOTE III. Before we notice a little more in detail the differences of these two characteristic formularies, it is desirable to set side by side the original Creed of the Council of Nicæa and the Constantinopolitan Creed which became for the West the popular authoritative embodiment of Nicene teaching.

THE NICENE CREED ('the Creed of the 318').

We believe

I. In One GOD the Father Almighty,
Maker
of all things both visible and invisible; and

II. In One Lord Jesus Christ,
the Son of GOD,
begotten of the Father,
only-begotten,
that is of the essence of the Father,
GOD of GOD,
Light of Light,
very GOD of very GOD,
begotten not made,
being of one essence with the Father,
through Whom all things were made
both the things in the heaven and the things in the earth.

THE CONSTANTINOPOLITAN CREED ('the Creed of the 150'). NOTE III.

We believe

I. In One GOD the Father Almighty,
Maker *of heaven and earth and*
of all things both visible and invisible; and

II. In One Lord Jesus Christ,
the only-begotten Son of GOD,
begotten of the Father *before all worlds (ages).*

Light of Light,
very GOD of very GOD,
begotten not made,
being of one essence with the Father,
through Whom all things were made.

NOTE III. Who for us men and for our salvation
came down and
was Incarnate,

was made man[1],

suffered, and

rose again the third day:

ascended into heaven, and

shall come
to judge the quick and the dead.

And

[1] The original word (ἐνανθρωπήσαντα) rather expresses the thought: 'lived among men Himself man' (1 Tim. ii. 5), '*tabernacled among us*' (John i. 14).

The word includes two distinct elements, the truth of the Lord's Manhood and the truth of His Human Life: and it is capable of two imperfect meanings, which in the course of controversy were actually given to it, the assumption of humanity and the dwelling with men. The Apollinarians denying the perfection of the Lord's Manhood insisted on the sense 'dwelt with men': the orthodox, in order to guard against this error, pressed exclusively the meaning 'united Himself with man,' i.e. took the fulness of manhood, body, soul and spirit. But it is obvious that it is as necessary to insist on the perfection of the Lord's Human Life as on the perfection of His Human Nature,

Who for us men and for our salvation NOTE III.
came down *from heaven*, and
was Incarnate
of the Holy Ghost and the Virgin Mary, and
was made man, *and*
was crucified for us under Pontius Pilate, and
suffered, and
was buried, and
rose again the third day
according to the Scriptures; and
ascended into heaven, *and*
sitteth on the right hand of the Father; and
he shall come *again with glory*
to judge the quick and the dead.
Whose kingdom shall have no end.
And

and that we have lost much by the neglect of this aspect of the Incarnation.

In the Creed of Cæsarea (Socr. *H. E.* 1, 8) the corresponding phrase was σαρκωθέντα καὶ ἐν ἀνθρώποις πολιτευσάμενον. These words fail to guard the thought of the perfect humanity which ἐνανθρωπήσαντα emphasises.

The patristic interpretation of ἐσκήνωσεν ἐν ἡμῖν failed exactly as their limited interpretation of ἐνανθρωπήσαντα.

The term ἐνανθρωπήσας is rendered *humanatus est* by Dionysius Exiguus in his translation of the Constantinopolitan Creed. In the Liturgical Latin texts the common rendering is *homo factus est*, but *humanatus est* and *inhumanatus est* are also found.

NOTE III. III. In the Holy Ghost[1].

On comparing these two Creeds it appears that the Constantinopolitan Creed does not contain three clauses which are contained in the Nicene :—

(1) *that is of the essence of the Father,*
(2) *GOD of GOD,*
(3) *both the things in the heaven and the things in the earth.*

[1] To this Confession the following anathema was added : 'But those that say that there was once when He was not, 'and that before He was begotten He was not, and that He 'came into being (ἐγένετο) from things that were not, or who 'affirm that the Son of God is of a different subsistence or 'essence, or created, subject to change or alteration, these 'men the Catholic and Apostolic Church anathematizes.'

In the translation of both Creeds I have followed what appears to be the best text without noticing small variations.

III. In the Holy Ghost, NOTE III.

the Lord, the Giver of life[1],

Who proceedeth from the Father,

Who with the Father and the Son together is worshipped and glorified,

Who spake through the prophets:

in one holy and catholic and apostolic Church.

We acknowledge

one Baptism for the remission of sins.

We look for

the Resurrection of the dead, and

the life of the world to come.

[1] τὸ κύριον, τὸ ζωοποιόν: *Dominum* et *vivificantem* (all. *vivificatorem*).

NOTE III. Of these the second was afterwards introduced into the Latin Version of the Creed; and the third corresponds in part with an additional clause in the first Article. But the first clause, on which stress was laid at Nicæa, never found any place in the Constantinopolitan formula.

On the other hand the Constantinopolitan Creed not only adds the clauses after 'the Holy Ghost,' which certainly existed in substance before the Council of Nicæa, but also gives several important phrases which found no place in the Nicene Creed:

(1) *of heaven and earth*, (2) *before all worlds*, (3) *from heaven*, (4) *of the Holy Ghost and the Virgin Mary*, (5) *crucified for us under Pontius Pilate*, (6) *buried*, (7) *according to the Scriptures*, (8) *sitteth on the right hand of the Father*, (9) *with glory*, (10) *whose kingdom shall have no end*[1].

It is obvious therefore that the Constantinopolitan Creed is a distinct formula from the Nicene Creed, though it includes one key-phrase of Nicæa 'of one essence with the Father.' The two Creeds were distinguished at the Council of Chalcedon where both were recited; but as early as the twelfth century at least the title 'Nicene' was applied to the 'Constantinopolitan' Creed, and so far with reason as the

[1] All these phrases are found in the first Creed of Epiphanius (A.D. 373); and all except (3), (4) and (7) literally or substantially in the Creed of Jerusalem (Hahn, *Bibl. d. Symb.* §§ 67, 62).

later formulary embodied in the simplest form the result gained by the Nicene Council. NOTE III.

In comparing the Eastern and Western Creeds one difference of expression, which has been obliterated in our own Service-books, will be noticed. The Eastern Creeds begin *We believe:* the Western *I believe:* and the Western usage was so influential that the singular form was introduced into the popular version of the Eastern Creed. The singular indeed is not unfrequent in the liturgical form of the symbol in the East; but it seems to be impossible not to recognise in the instinct which gave shape to the Western Creed a trace of that consciousness of individual responsibility, of direct personal confession, which from age to age has given a fresh character to Western Christianity.

If now we turn to the types of the Eastern and Western Creed as represented in our Western formularies it will be seen that the fundamental difference between them which has been briefly characterised, finds expression in each of the three great Articles which they contain. In the Eastern Creeds the Father is described emphatically as *One*, and as the Maker of heaven and earth, *of all things visible and invisible*. The unity of the Godhead, the fact of Creation by the Supreme GOD and not by a rival Demiurge, the existence and functions of the beings of the spiritual world, had a significance in Eastern speculation which was unrealised in the West. And

NOTE III. so it came to pass that these three points are distinctly touched upon in the Eastern Creeds, while two of them are passed over in the Western Creeds and the third obtained general recognition in them only at a late date. The epithet *One*, which occurs in the earliest types of the Western Creed (Irenæus, Tertullian) as a part of the apostolic outline, actually dropped out afterwards. The glimpse opened into the unseen world by the words *all things visible and invisible*, does not seem ever to have found a place in a Western Creed. And the clause *Maker of heaven and earth*, which is found substantially in Irenæus and Tertullian, does not occur in the Roman or Aquileian forms of the Creed, nor indeed till the middle of the seventh century, from which time it obtained general currency.

The differences are still more conspicuous in the second Article. The Western Creeds contain no trace of that description of the Nature and Work of the Son before the Incarnation which is the very heart of the Eastern Creeds. All is summed up in the title *Jesus Christ His only Son our Lord.* The Western fathers seem to have shrunk from expressing in words the Truth which they held implicitly. The Eastern on the other hand heaped up phrase on phrase, if so they might make clear what they had realised in painful controversy. Each of the seven clauses as they are recited—*Begotten of the Father before all worlds, GOD of GOD, Light of Light, Very GOD of Very*

GOD, begotten not made, being of one substance (coessential) *with the Father, through Whom all things were made,*—recalls a conflict and consecrates a truth won through struggles in which the West had no independent share. There is also the same striving after doctrinal fulness of expression in the Eastern paragraph on the Incarnation as in that on the essential Being of the Son. Nothing in the Western Creeds corresponds with the words: *Who for us men and for our salvation came down [from heaven] and was made man.* The Constantinopolitan addition *crucified for us* shews the same feeling. The other phrases peculiar to the Constantinopolitan Creed *of the Holy Ghost and the Virgin Mary, according to the Scriptures* and *of whose kingdom shall be no end,* were probably due to local causes. This first was probably pointed at the Apollinarian heresy, and the last is said to have been directed against the false teaching of Marcellus of Ancyra. On the other hand the Western Creed of Aquileia introduced a clause which never found a place in any of the orthodox Eastern Creeds; *Descended into Hell (Hades) (descendit ad inferna).* This difference is perhaps more worthy of notice because the *Descent into the world below* forms a very prominent topic in the account of the preaching of Thaddæus to Abgarus said to have been preserved at Edessa. NOTE III.

In the third article the differences are not less significant. Nothing is said in the Western Creeds

NOTE III. of the Personal Nature or Work of the Holy Spirit. Here again the implicit Faith of the Church is gathered up in words which were never changed and never developed, *I believe in the Holy Ghost.* It was late before the epithet *Catholic* was added to the phrase *the Holy Church;* and the remaining epithets *One* and *Apostolic* are peculiar to the Eastern Creeds. It is perhaps surprising that the connexion of *baptism* with the *remission of sins* should be found in the Eastern but not in the Western Creeds, though this is probably due to the influence of the earliest apostolic type which was preserved unchanged in the East. But no clause could more completely answer to the spirit of the West than that which is the peculiar glory of the Western Creed, the clause which teaches us to regard the whole Church, the whole Body of Christ, as *a Communion of Saints,* opening in this way a new vision of the unseen order from the side of a common and abiding life. And perhaps we may connect this clause with the other clause which we have noticed as characteristic of the West: *He descended into Hades* (*the world below*). The fellowship which Christ has brought reaches through the past and not through the future only: the blessings of redemption are shewn to have an entrance, how we cannot even rudely imagine, to realms of being beyond the experience of our present life.

One further reflection offers itself after this rapid survey of the general differences of the Eastern and

Western Creeds. The Eastern Creeds were from NOTE III. their very construction more flexible than the Western. There are in the former great varieties of filling up within the same outline. In the latter four new clauses and six new words were added in the course of time, but in general expression the earliest Roman Creed (that of Marcellus of Ancyra) is identical with the latest.

The Eastern Creeds have, as we have seen, a distinctly dogmatic character. They not only record facts, like the Western Creeds, but interpret them. This tendency is seen most fully in the Nicene Creed where three phrases at once arrest attention: *only-begotten* (μονογενής), *of the essence of the Father* (ἐκ τῆς οὐσίας τοῦ πατρός), *of one essence with the Father* (ὁμοούσιος). Of these the first and third have found a place in our own popular Confession. Together they are sufficient to preserve the full integrity of the ancient belief without seeming to intrude into regions inaccessible by human thought. The first guards the thought of the unique Personality, and the last the thought of the essential Deity of the Son. We require to be assured that God is brought near to us, to our whole being; and we require to be assured that this knowledge of God which is thus given to us is not illusory.

On the other hand each term by itself is open to misrepresentation.

If we rest in the thought of 'the only Son' and

NOTE III. try to pursue that thought alone to the remoter consequences which seem to be involved in it, we find ourselves met by difficulties which belong to the ideas of beginning, of material existence, of separate individuality. If again we think of coessentiality only, then little by little the conception of three distinct, eternal Persons in the one God fades away. There is on the one side of the twofold Truth an affinity, if I may so speak, to the modes of thought which issue in Arianism (the 'dividing the Divine substance' 'essence'), and on the other side an affinity to the modes of thought which issue in Sabellianism (the 'confounding the Divine Persons'). Perhaps we may go one step further and say that Arianism and Sabellianism represent within the circle of Christian knowledge the final issues of an unbelieving Judaism and a completed Heathenism, that is theism and pantheism, the separation of God from the world and the confusion of God with the world. So much at least is certain, disastrous results answering to these typical forms of error follow from an exclusive development of one side or other of the complex Truth; but if we keep both sides before us we may hope to attain, so far as the end is within our reach, to that knowledge of the whole Truth which belongs to man.

NOTE IV.

THE DIVINE FATHERHOOD.

No one knoweth the Son, save the Father; neither doth any know the Father, save the Son, and he to whomsoever the Son willeth to reveal Him.

MATT. xi. 27.

THE idea of the Divine Fatherhood answering to that of human sonship and childship, is gradually unfolded in the Bible. NOTE IV

"In the Old Testament the general notion of Fatherhood was made personal by the special covenants which He was pleased to establish with representative men. He thus became the 'Father' of the chosen people in a peculiar sense (Ex. iv. 22; Deut. xxxii. 6; comp. i. 31, viii. 5; Is. lxiii. 16, lxiv. 8; comp. xliii. 1, 6, 21, xliv. 2, 24, xlvi. 3 ff.; Jer. xxxi. 9, 20; Hos. xi. 1; Mal. ii. 10; comp. i. 6); and each member of the nation was His child (Deut. xiv. 1; Is. i. 2, xxx. 1, 9, xliii. 6, lxiii. 8; Jer. iii. 4, 19; comp. Matt. xv. 24, 26). But this sonship was regarded as an exceptional blessing. It belonged to the nation as 'priests and kings' to the Lord; and so we find that the relationship of privilege, in which all the children of Israel shared in some manner, was in an especial degree the characteristic of the theocratic minister (comp. Ps. lxxxii. 6). Of the king the representative head of the royal nation, GOD said '*Thou art my Son, this day,*'

NOTE IV. that is at the moment of the solemn consecration, '*have I begotten thee*' (Ps. ii. 7): and again, '*He shall cry unto me: Thou art my Father, my GOD, and the rock of my salvation. Also I will make him my first-born, higher than the kings of the earth*' (Ps. lxxxix. 26 f.; comp. 2 Sam. vii. 12 ff.). Comp. Ecclus. xxiii. 1, 4.

"It will however be observed on a study of the passages that the idea of Fatherhood in the Old Testament is determined by the conceptions of an Eastern household, and further that it is nowhere extended to men generally. GOD is the great Head of the family which looks back to Him as its Author. His 'children' owe Him absolute obedience and reverence: they are 'in His hand': and conversely He offers them wise counsel and protection. But the ruling thought throughout is that of authority and not of love. The relationship is derived from a peculiar manifestation of GOD's Providence to one race (Ex. iv. 22; Hos. xi. 1), and not from the original connexion of man as man with GOD. If the nobility of sonship is to be extended to Gentiles, it is by their incorporation in the chosen family (Ps. lxxxvii.).

"So far the conception of a divine Fatherhood is (broadly speaking) national among the Jews as it was physical in the Gentile world. But in the Gospels the idea of Sonship is spiritual and personal. GOD is revealed as the Giver and Sustainer (Matt. vii. 9 ff.) of a life like His own, to those who were created in

His image, after His likeness, but who have been alienated from Him (Luke xv. 11 ff.). The original capacity of man to receive God is declared, and at the same time the will of God to satisfy it. Both facts are set forth once for all in the person of Him who was both the Son of man and the Son of God. NOTE IV.

"The idea of the divine Fatherhood and of the divine Sonship as realised in Christ appears in His first recorded words and in His dedication to His public ministry. The words spoken in the Temple: '*Wist ye not that I must be in my Father's house?*' (Luke ii. 49 ἐν τοῖς τοῦ πατρός) appear to mark in the Lord, from the human side, the quickened consciousness of His mission at a crisis of His life, while as yet the local limitations of worship are fully recognised (contrast John iv. 21). The voice of the Baptism declares decisively the authority of acknowledged Sonship as that in which He is to accomplish His work (Matt. iii. 17 and parallels; comp. John i. 34).

"In the Sermon on the Mount the idea of God's Fatherhood in relation both to Christ and to the disciples is exhibited most prominently. The first notice of the sonship of men is remarkable and if rightly interpreted most significant: '*Blessed are the peacemakers for they shall be called sons of God*' (Matt. v. 9). This benediction is seen in its true light by comparison with the angelic hymn: '*On earth peace among men of well-pleasing*' (Luke ii. 14). The peace of which Christ speaks is that of reunited humanity (comp. Eph.

NOTE IV. ii. 14 ff.). The blessing of sonship is for those who, quickened by GOD's Spirit (Rom. viii. 14), help to realise on earth that inward brotherhood of which He has given the foundation and the pledge.

"The teaching which follows the beatitude enforces and unfolds this thought. The sign of Sonship is to be found in GOD-like works which cannot but be referred at once to their true and heavenly origin (Matt. v. 16). These are to be in range no less universal than the most universal gifts of GOD, the rain and the sunshine (v. 44 ff.; Luke vi. 35 ff.), in order that the fulness of divine Sonship may be attained and manifested (*v.* 45; Luke vi. 35). At the same time the standard of judgment, even all-knowing love, impresses a new character upon action (Matt. vi. 1, 4, 6, 18). The obligations of kindred to others follow from the privilege of kindred with the common Father (Matt. vi. 14 f.; Mark xi. 25 f.). The Father's knowledge anticipates the petitions of the children (Matt. vi. 8; Luke xii. 30), and duly provides for their wants (Matt. vi. 26 ff.; Luke xii. 24). Here and elsewhere the laws of natural affection are extended to spiritual relations (Matt. vii. 9 ff.; Luke xi. 11 ff.).

"From these passages it will be seen how immeasurably the conception of Fatherhood is extended by the Lord beyond that in the Old Testament. The bond is moral, and not physical: it is personal and human, and not national. It suggests thoughts of character, of duty, of confidence, which belong to a believer as such and not peculiarly to those who stand in particular outward circumstances. In the few other passages in the Synoptic Gospels in which the title 'your Father' occurs, it has the same force: it conveys implicitly grounds of trust and the certainty of future triumph (Matt. x. 10, 29; Luke xii. 32). The 'name' of Him whom the Lord made known was, it may be said truly, 'the Father,' even as the name of Him Who sent Moses was 'Jehovah,' 'the absolute,' 'the self-existent[1].' And in this connexion the first petition of the Lord's Prayer gains a new meaning: *Our Father which art in heaven, hallowed be Thy name*, —the supreme revelation of Fatherhood (Matt. vi. 9; comp. Luke xi. 2). NOTE IV.

"The revelation of the Father is indeed distinctly claimed by the Lord for Himself alone (Matt. xi. 27; Luke x. 22). True discipleship to Him is the fulfilment of 'His Father's' will (Matt. vii. 21). He pronounces with authority upon the divine counsels and the divine working, as being of 'His Father' (Matt. xv. 13, xvi. 17, xviii. 10, 14, 19, 35, xxv. 34, xxvi. 29; Luke xxii. 29). He speaks of 'His Father's promise' (Luke xxiv. 49), and of 'His Father's presence' (Matt. x. 32 f.) with the confidence of a Son.

[1] Or perhaps 'He who maketh to be.' There is really no strict representative of the name Jehovah in the New Testament except in the ὁ ὤν of the Apocalypse, and even there it is modified: Apoc. i. 4, 8, iv. 8 (ὁ ὢν καὶ ὁ ἦν καὶ ὁ ἐρχ.), xi. 17, xvi. 5 (ὁ ὢν καὶ ὁ ἦν).

NOTE IV. But with the confidence of a Son the Lord maintains also the dependence of a Son. Every prayer which He makes will be answered (Matt. xxvi. 53), yet He places Himself wholly in 'His Father's' hands (Matt. xxvi. 39, 42); and He reserves some things for His Father alone (Matt. xx. 23).

"Such a revelation of the divine Fatherhood through the Son to sons definitely distinguishes the Christian doctrine of GOD from Pantheism and Theism. As against Pantheism it shews GOD as distinct from and raised immeasurably above the world; as against Theism it shews GOD as entering into a living fellowship with men, as taking humanity into personal union with Himself. The unseen King of the divine Kingdom is made known as One to whom His people can draw near with the confidence of children.

"The revelation of GOD as the Father is specially brought out by St John; but in a somewhat different form from that in which it is found in the Synoptists. Two titles occur commonly in the Gospel in relation to Christ: (α) the Father; and (β) My Father. Both of these occur in the Synoptists each nine or ten times. But on the other hand St John never uses the phrases *My* (*your*) *Father in heaven* (*heavenly Father*) which occur each nine times in the Synoptic Gospels; nor does he use the phrase *your Father* except xx. 17 (in contrast); nor yet the Pauline phrase *our Father* in his own writings. In the Epistles he uses uniformly the absolute title *the Father* (comp. 2 John 3) without any addition; and in the Apocalypse *His* (*My*) *Father* but not *the Father*. NOTE IV.

"These differences though minute are really significant. St John in his latest writings regards the relation of the Divine Fatherhood in its eternal, that is, in its present, realisation, and not in regard to another order. Or to look at the truth from another point of view, St John presents to us the Sonship of Christ, the foundation of the sonship of men, from its absolute side, while the Synoptists connect it with the fulfilment of the office of the Messianic King[1]."

These general remarks will probably be sufficient to lead the student to examine the characteristic teaching of St Paul upon the subject.

[1] Additional Note on 1 John i. 2.

NOTE V.

All-sovereign and Almighty.

Unto the King of the ages, incorruptible, invisible, the only GOD, *be honour and glory for ever and ever.*

1 TIM. i. 17.

Of Him, and through Him, and unto Him, are all things.

ROM. xi. 36.

THE title 'Almighty' came into our version of the Creed, and generally into our Collects, from the Latin 'omnipotens,' which fails altogether to express the term παντοκράτωρ 'all-sovereign' which occupies the corresponding place in the earliest Greek writings. This word παντοκράτωρ is apparently of Biblical origin and is almost if not wholly confined to writings influenced by Biblical language. It occurs in the LXX. in the phrase κύριος παντοκράτωρ, which is the rendering of Jehovah Sabáoth ('the Lord of Hosts') in a large group of books of the O. T., and again as a rendering of Shaddai ('the Almighty') in Job. It is found also several times in the Apocrypha (Ecclus. xlii. 17, L. 14, 17; Wisd. vii. 25); and in Philo. It occurs frequently in the Apocalypse (i. 8, iv. 8 &c.) and in 2 Cor. vi. 18 in a quotation from the LXX. (2 Sam. vii. 8). NOTE V.

The word παντοδύναμος, which is the true equivalent to *omnipotens*, is not found either in the Greek versions of the Old Testament or in the New Testament; but it occurs three times in the book of

NOTE V. Wisdom (vii. 23, xi. 18, xviii. 15), once in close connexion with παντοκράτωρ (vii. 23, 25).

ap. Clem. Alex. *Ecl. Proph. fragm.* §26, p. 996.

Both words παντοκράτωρ and παντοδύναμος are used together of GOD in a remarkable passage of THEODOTUS, and the two divine attributes, 'all-sovereignty' and 'almightiness' are discussed at length by the PSEUDO-DIONYSIUS; but, as far as I have noticed, παντοδύναμος does not occur in any original Greek Creed, though it is found in Greek translations of the Apostles' Creed[1].

Notwithstanding the clear difference between the moral conception of universal dominion (παντοκράτωρ) and the metaphysical conception of omnipotence (παντοδύναμος) the Latin Versions seem to give *omnipotens*

[1] It is worthy of notice that in the Greek translation of the Apostles' Creed found in the 'Psalter of Gregory' in the Library of Corpus Christi College, Cambridge (Sæc. xv.) the word '*omnipotens*' is rendered by the actual equivalent παντοκράτωρ in the first article, and in the later clause by παντοδύναμος, when the translator had no parallel Greek clause to guide him. In other copies of the Greek version παντοδύναμος and παντοκράτωρ occur severally in both places. See Hahn, *Bibl. d. Symb.* pp. 59 ff.: Caspari, *Ungedr. Quellen*, iii. 209 ff.

In the old English translation of the Creed contained in the great Eadwine Psalter in the Library of Trinity College (R. 17) there is a similar difference between the renderings in the two places. In the first clause *omnipotens* is translated 'aelwealdend,' and in the later clause 'ealmihtig,' which is also given as an alternative in the former place. On the other hand in a Royal MS. of the British Museum (Cleop. B. vi.) the rendering in the first place is 'Hal-michttende' and in the second place 'al-waldand' (comp. Heurtley, *Harm. Symb.* pp. 87, 91, 94).

universally as the rendering of παντοκράτωρ in the N.T. and in the Creed. There is however a trace of another rendering *omnitenens* in Augustine (*De Gen. ad lit.* iv. 12, § 22): Creatoris potentia et omnipotentis atque omnitenentis virtus causa subsistendi est omni creaturæ, quæ virtus ab eis quæ creata sunt regendis si aliquando cessaret, simul et illorum cessaret species, omnisque natura concideret: just as Tertullian translates κοσμοκράτορες (Eph. vi. 12) 'world-rulers' by *munditenentes* (*adv. Marc.* v. 18). NOTE V.

This latter interpretation of the word (*omnitenens*) answers in part to the interpretation of the Greek Fathers. Thus THEOPHILUS in explaining the different titles of GOD says: 'He is called παντοκράτωρ because 'He holds all things and embraces them (τὰ πάντα 'κρατεῖ καὶ ἐμπεριέχει). For the heights of the heavens 'and the depths of the abysses and the ends of the 'earth are in His hand and there is no place for His 'rest' (Is. lxvi. 1). *ad Autol.* i. 4.

CYRIL OF JERUSALEM explains the word at length and points its force against those who held false views about the material universe. 'The heretics,' he says, 'know not One All-sovereign GOD. For "all-'sovereign" (παντοκράτωρ) is He who sways all, who 'has authority over all (ὁ πάντων κρατῶν, ὁ πάντων 'ἐξουσιάζων). But they that say that one is Lord of 'the soul and some other of the body, say that 'neither of them is perfect, by the fact that one part 'is lacking to each. For he that hath authority over *Catech.* viii. 3.

NOTE V. 'the soul but hath no authority over the body, how 'is he All-sovereign? and he that is lord over bodies 'but hath no authority over spirits, how is he All-'sovereign?'

c. Eunom. ii. Migne *Patr. Gr.* xlv. p. 524. GREGORY OF NYSSA in the course of his interpretation of the title says: 'Just as there would have 'been no physician had there been no sick...so there 'would have been no Universal Sovereign unless all 'the Creation had required One to exercise sovereignty 'over it and keep it in being...Therefore whenever 'we hear the word "All-sovereign" we have this 'thought that GOD holds together all things in being, 'both things intelligible and things material. For it is 'for this reason He holds the circle of the earth, for 'this reason He keeps in His hand the ends of the 'earth, for this reason He encloses the heaven with 'His span, for this reason He measures the water 'with His hand, for this reason He embraces all the 'intelligible creation in Himself, that all things may 'remain in being since they are swayed by His em-'bracing power' (τῇ περιεκτικῇ δυνάμει περικρατούμενα).

This general interpretation was so widely spread that in spite of the rendering *omnipotens* the true conception of παντοκράτωρ 'all-sovereign' remained *in Symb.* § 5. for some time in the Latin Church. Thus RUFFINUS explains *omnipotens* as expressing GOD's 'dominion over all' (omnipotens ab eo dicitur quod omnium *de Trin.* c. 2. teneat potentatum). And at an earlier time NOVATIAN gave expression to the substance of Greek thought when he thus wrote of the 'omnipotence' of GOD: 'He himself over everything, holding all things, 'leaving nothing unoccupied outside Himself, hath 'yielded no room (as some fancy) to any superior Deity. 'Inasmuch as He hath embraced all things together 'in the bosom of His perfect greatness and power, 'ever intent upon His own work and penetrating 'through everything, and moving all things, and 'quickening all together, and beholding the whole, 'and so combining into harmony the discordant sub-'stances of all the elements, that the one world 'formed of diverse elements is so firmly framed by that 'close and vital union, that it cannot be dissolved by 'any force till He alone Who made gives the word for 'its dissolution that He may shew us other greater 'works.' NOTE V.

But this thought of the all-sustaining power of GOD only gives one side of His universal sovereignty. The word παντοκράτωρ represents Him also as ruling all things for the fulfilment of His will. He is not only Creator and Preserver, but yet more 'the King of the Ages' (ὁ βασιλεὺς τῶν αἰώνων, *rex sæculorum* V.[1]) through Whose dominion the end of Creation is attained step by step, in the vast succession of dispensations (comp. Hebr. xi. 3, πίστει νοοῦμεν κατηρτίσθαι τοὺς αἰῶνας ῥήματι Θεοῦ). 1 Tim. i. 17.

[1] It is worthy of notice that this very phrase 'rex sæculorum' is introduced into the African Creed of Augustine and of Fulgentius of Ruspe: Hahn, *Bibl. d. Symb.* pp. 30, 33.

NOTE V. *Serm.* xl. § 45. So GREGORY OF NAZIANZUS in a summary exposition of the Creed in connexion with Baptism explains the first clause: 'Believe that the whole world, all 'that is seen and all that is unseen, was made of GOD '(*παρὰ θεοῦ γενόμενον*) out of that which was not, and 'that, administered by the providence of Him who 'made it, it receives its change to the better (*τὴν εἰς 'τὸ κρεῖττον μεταβολήν*).'

In this respect the title 'All-sovereign' *παντοκράτωρ* stands in a significant contrast to *κοσμοκράτωρ* 'world-sovereign,' which is applied to adverse powers, who hold at present a partial and permitted (Luke iv. 6) sway. So Scripture recognises the disorder of the world as it falls under our present observation but points to a larger view and an ultimate fulfilment of life which corresponds with the perfect will of GOD. (Eph. vi. 12.)

It was fortunate that the Greek translation of the Creed gave occasion to Pearson to dwell upon the 'all-sovereignty' of GOD as distinct from His 'almightiness'; but it has been a great loss to popular theology that an abstract conception of infinite power has commonly taken the place of the Biblical revelation of the actual dominion of GOD over all that He has made. (*On the Creed*, pp. 42 ff.)

NOTE VI.

The Christology of the New Testament.

The Advocate, even the Holy Spirit whom the Father will send in My name, He shall teach you all things.

JOHN xiv. 26.

NOTE VI.

NO exercise can give a more vivid impression of the historical truth and unity of the writings of the New Testament than an investigation of the gradual unfolding of the teaching on the Person of Christ which they contain in connexion with the circumstances under which the several statements are given. In the early chapters of the Acts, for example, it is possible to see how the Apostles were enabled step by step, under the guidance of the Spirit, to apprehend naturally (so to speak) the divine character of Him with Whom they had 'companied' as men with Man. On the other hand it is impossible to understand how any one writing first when the belief of the Church was already shaped could have traced the successive phases through which it passed in the first days. The record is evidently a direct transcript from life.

In studying the subject the student should consider the self-revelation of the Lord as given in the history of the Gospels, and then the Apostles' announcement of the Christ in their preaching and in their epistles.

NOTE VI. A brief outline of a plan of inquiry which has been found useful is all that can be given here.

I. The self-revelation of the Lord.

i. In the Synoptists.

(*a*) To the confession of St Peter at Cæsarea Philippi.

(*b*) From St Peter's confession to the Ascension.

ii. In St John.

(*a*) The revelation to the world (i. 19—xii. 50).

(*b*) The revelation to the disciples (xiii.—xxi.).

II. Titles accepted or used by our Lord.

(*a*) The Son of David.

(*b*) The Christ.

(*c*) The Son of GOD.

(*d*) The Son of man.

(*e*) The Son.

III. The apostolic announcement.

i. The testimony of the apostles of the circumcision.

(*a*) *Acts* i.—xii. The preaching of St Peter.

(*b*) *The Epistle of St James.*

(*c*) *The first Epistle of St Peter* (2 *Peter*, *Jude*).

The central thought in this group of writings is that Jesus of Nazareth is the Christ of prophecy.

The first Epistle of St Peter forms a transition to the writings of St Paul; and the whole group leads up to the Epistle to the Hebrews. NOTE VI.

ii. The testimony of St Paul.

(*a*) *Acts* xiii.—xxviii. The preaching of St Paul.

(*b*) The Epistles.

(1) 1, 2 *Thessalonians.*

(2) 1, 2 *Corinthians, Galatians, Romans.*

(3) The Epistles of the Captivity to Churches (*Philippians, Colossians, Ephesians*).

(4) The personal letters (1, 2 *Timothy, Titus, Philemon*).

In these the central thought is that of the Ascended and glorified Christ.

iii. The testimony on the eve of the Coming.

(*a*) *The Epistle to the Hebrews.*

(*b*) *The Apocalypse.*

In these Christ is shewn, under two aspects, to offer the ideal fulfilment of all the divine promises.

iv. The testimony of the New Church.

The Epistles of St John.

The Gospel of St John (i. 1—18).

The revelation of the Eternal, Immanent, Incarnate Word.

In the following five passages the student will find a view of Christ's person and Work in the chief aspects.

NOTE VI. I. The teaching of ST PAUL.

i. *The Son in self-humiliation; Jesus in exaltation:* Phil. ii. 5—11.

ii. *The Son in relation to all created being:* Col. i. 15—20.

iii. *Christ and the believer:* Eph. i. 3—14.

II. The teaching of the EPISTLE TO THE HEBREWS.

The Son and humanity (fallen man): Hebr. ii. 5—18.

III. The teaching of ST JOHN.

The Word and the Word Incarnate: i. 1—18.

NOTE VII.

The Universality of the Character of the Lord.

Come unto Me, all ye that labour and are heavy laden, and I will give you rest.

MATT. xi. 28.

If any man thirst, let him come unto Me and drink.

JOHN vii. 37.

I am the vine, ye are the branches.

JOHN xv. 5.

MR Goldwin Smith has given in a Lecture *On some supposed Consequences of the Doctrine of Historical Progress*, a view of the moral evidence for the Gospel furnished by the Character of the Lord which deserves the most careful attention[1]. A few extracts will be sufficient to shew the insight and breadth of sympathy with which the study is drawn. NOTE VII.

"The Type of Character set forth in the Gospel history is an absolute embodiment of Love both in the way of action and affection, crowned by the highest possible exhibition of it in an act of the most transcendent self-devotion to the interest of the human race. This being the case, it is difficult to see how the Christian morality can ever be brought into antagonism with the moral progress of mankind; or how the Christian type of Character can ever be left behind by the course of human development, lose the allegiance of the moral world, or give place to a newly emerging and higher ideal. This type, it

[1] Mr Goldwin Smith has re-stated and illustrated part of the argument in the *Contemporary Review* for *December*, 1883.

NOTE VII. would appear, being perfect, will be final. It will be final, not as precluding future history, but as comprehending it. The moral efforts of all ages, to the consummation of the world, will be efforts to realise this character, and to make it actually, as it is potentially, universal. While these efforts are being carried on under all the various circumstances of life and society, and under all the various moral and intellectual conditions attaching to particular men, an infinite variety of characters, personal and national, will be produced; a variety ranging from the highest human grandeur down to the very verge of the grotesque. But these characters, with all their variations, will go beyond their source and their ideal only as the rays of light go beyond the sun. Humanity, as it passes through phase after phase of the historical movement, may advance indefinitely in excellence; but its advance will be an indefinite approximation to the Christian Type. A divergence from that type, to whatever extent it may take place, will not be progress, but debasement and corruption. In a moral point of view, in short, the world may abandon Christianity, but it can never advance beyond it. This is not a matter of authority, or even of Revelation. If it is true, it is a matter of reason as much as anything in the world.

"There are many peculiarities arising out of personal and historical circumstances, which are incident to the best human characters, and which would prevent any one of them from being universal or final as a type. But the Type set up in the Gospels as the Christian Type seems to have escaped all these peculiarities, and to stand out in unapproached purity as well as in unapproached perfection of moral excellence. NOTE VII.

"The good moral characters which we see among men fall, speaking broadly, into two general classes; those which excite our reverence and those which excite our love. ......

"Now, if the type proposed in the Gospels for our imitation were characteristically noble or characteristically amiable, characteristically grand or characteristically beautiful, it might have great moral attractions, but it would not be universal or final. It would belong to one peculiar hemisphere of character, and even though man might not yet actually have transcended it, the ideal would lie beyond it; it would not remain for ever the mark and goal of our moral progress. But the fact is, it is neither characteristically noble and grand, nor characteristically amiable and beautiful; but both in an equal degree, perfectly and indistinguishably, the fusion of the two classes of qualities being complete, so that the mental eye, though it be strained to aching, cannot discern whether that on which it gazes be more the object of reverence or of love.

"There are differences again between the male and female character, under which, nevertheless, we

NOTE VII. divine that there lies a real identity, and a consequent tendency to fusion in the ultimate ideal. Had the Gospel type of character been stamped with the peculiar marks of either sex, we should have felt that there was an ideal free from those peculiarities beyond it. But this is not the case. It exhibits, indeed, the peculiarly male virtue of courage in the highest degree, and in the form in which it is most clear of mere animal impetuosity and most evidently a virtue; but this form is the one common to both sexes, as the annals of martyrdom prove. ......

"There is an equally notable absence of any of the peculiarities which attend particular callings and modes of life, and which, though so inevitable under the circumstances of human society, that we have learnt to think them beauties, would disqualify a Character for being universal and the ideal. The Life depicted in the Gospel is one of pure beneficence, disengaged from all peculiar social circumstances, yet adapted to all. ......

"The Christian Type of Character, if it was constructed by human intellect, was constructed at the confluence of three races, the Jewish, the Greek, and the Roman, each of which had strong national peculiarities of its own. A single touch, a single taint of any one of these peculiarities, and the character would have been national, not universal; transient, not eternal: it might have been the highest character in history, but it would have been disqualified for being the ideal. Supposing it to have been human, whether it were the effort of a real man to attain moral excellence, or a moral imagination of the writers of the Gospels, the chances, surely, were infinite against its escaping any tincture of the fanaticism, formalism, and exclusiveness of the Jew, of the political pride of the Roman, of the intellectual pride of the Greek. Yet it has entirely escaped them all. NOTE VII.

"Historical circumstances affect character sometimes directly, sometimes by way of reaction. The formalism of the Pharisees might have been expected to drive any character with which it was brought into collision into the opposite extreme of laxity; yet no such effect can be discerned. Antinomianism is clearly a deflection from the Christian pattern, and the offspring of a subsequent age.

"The political circumstances of Judæa, as a country suffering from the oppression of foreign conquerors, were calculated to produce in the oppressed Jews either insurrectionary violence (which was constantly breaking out) or the dull apathy of Oriental submission. But the Life which is the example of Christians escaped both these natural impressions. It was an active and decisive attack on the evils of the age; but the attack was directed not against political tyranny or its agents, but against the moral corruption which was its source. ......

"The essence of man's moral nature, clothed with a personality so vivid and intense as to excite through

NOTE VII. all ages the most intense affection, yet divested of all those peculiar characteristics, the accidents of place and time, by which human personalities are marked, —what other notion than this can philosophy form of Divinity manifest on earth?"

Lectures on the Study of History, pp. 133—142.
Oxford, 1865.

NOTE VIII.

The Blood of Christ.

The blood of Jesus His Son cleanseth us from all sin.

1 JOHN i. 7.

The blood is the life.

DEUT. xii. 23.

"THE interpretation of the passages in the New Testament which refer to the blessings obtained by the 'Blood' of Christ must rest finally upon the interpretation given to the use of Blood in the sacrificial system of the O. T. Our own natural associations with Blood tend, if not to mislead, at least to obscure the ideas which it suggested to a Jew. NOTE VIII.

"And here it is obvious that the place occupied by Blood in the Jewish sacrifices was connected with the general conception attached to it throughout the Pentateuch. The Blood is the seat of Life in such a sense that it can be spoken of directly as the Life itself (Gen. ix. 4; Deut. xii. 23). More exactly the Life is said to be 'in the Blood' (Lev. xvii. 11). Hence it was forbidden to eat flesh with the blood (Gen. ix. 4; Lev. vii. 26 f.; xvii. 11 ff.; Deut. xii. 23 f.); a man might not use another's life for the support of his physical life.

"For it must be observed that by the outpouring of the Blood the life which was in it was not destroyed, though it was separated from the organism which it

NOTE VIII. had before quickened (Gen. iv. 10; comp. Hebr. xii. 24; Apoc. vi. 10).

"This prohibition of the use of Blood as food gave occasion for the clearest declaration of its significance in sacrifice: *I will even set my face against that soul that eateth blood, and will cut him off from among the people. For the soul (life) of the flesh is in the blood; and I have given it to you upon the altar to make an atonement for your souls (lives), for the Blood it atones through the soul (life)*, i.e. its atoning virtue lies not in its material substance but in the life of which it is the 'vehicle' (Lev. xvii. 10 f.). Moreover, the Blood already shed is distinctly treated as living. When it is sprinkled 'upon the altar' it makes atonement in virtue of the 'life' which is in it.

"Thus two distinct ideas were included in the sacrifice of a victim, the death of the victim by the shedding of its blood, and the liberation, so to speak, of the principle of life by which it had been animated, so that this life became available for another end. The ritual of sacrifice took account of both these moments in the symbolic act. The slaughtering of the victim, which was properly the work of the offerer, was sharply separated from the sprinkling of the blood which was the exclusive work of the priest. The death was inflicted by him who in his representative acknowledged the due punishment of his sin; the bringing near to GOD of the life so rendered up was the office of the appointed mediators between GOD and men. Death and life were both exhibited, death as NOTE VIII the consequence of sin, and life made by the Divine appointment a source of life. And it is worthy of notice that these two thoughts of the shedding and of the sprinkling of the Blood, which embrace the two elements in the conception of atonement were equally expressed by one word rendered *outpouring of blood* (Hebr. ix. 22, αἱματεκχυσία). Thus the life was first surrendered and then united with God.

"So far the thoughts suggested by the Jewish animal sacrifices seem to be clear; but they were necessarily imperfect and transitional. The union between the offerer and the offering was conventional and not real. The victim was irrational, so that there could be no true fellowship between it and the offender. Its death was involuntary, so that it could not embody in the highest form surrender to the Divine will.

"All that was foreshadowed by the Mosaic sacrificial system, all that was from the nature of the case wanting in it, Christ supplied. With Him, the Son of Man, all men are made capable of vital union: in Him all men find their true life. His sacrifice of Himself, through life and through death, was in every part a reasonable service; He endured the Cross at the hands of men; He was at once 'offered' and 'offered himself' (Hebr. ix. 14, 28): *and by His own blood He entered in into the holy place, having obtained eternal redemption for us* (Hebr. ix. 12).

NOTE VIII. "Thus in accordance with the typical teaching of the Levitical ordinances the Blood of Christ represents Christ's Life (1) as rendered in free self-sacrifice to GOD for men, and (2) as brought into perfect fellowship with GOD, having been set free by death. The Blood of Christ is, as shed, the Life of Christ given for men, and, as offered, the Life of Christ now given to men, the Life which is the spring of their life (John xii. 24). In each case the efficacy of the Life of Christ depends, from man's side, on the incorporation of the believer 'in Christ.'

"It will be evident from what has been said that while the thought of Christ's Blood (as shed) includes all that is involved in Christ's Death, the Death of Christ, on the other hand, expresses only a part, the initial part, of the whole conception of Christ's Blood. The Blood always includes the thought of the life preserved and active beyond death.

"This conception of the Blood of Christ is fully brought out in the fundamental passage, John vi. 53—56. Participation in Christ's Blood is participation in His life (*v.* 56). But at the same time it is implied throughout that it is only through His Death—His violent Death—that His Blood can be made available for men.

"In the other passages of St John's writings, where reference is made to the Blood of Christ, now one part of the whole conception and now the other predominates. In Apoc. i. 5, *unto Him that loveth us, and loosed us from our sins by his blood*, and in Apoc. v. 9, *Thou wast slain, and didst purchase unto GOD with thy blood*, the idea of the single act, the pouring out of blood in death, is most prominent and yet not exclusively present. In the one case the present participle (*Him that loveth*) seems to extend the act beyond the moment of accomplishment; and in the other *with* (*in*) *Thy blood* is felt to add something to *was slain* which is not included in it. The Blood is not simply the price by which the redeemed were purchased but the power by which they were quickened so as to be capable of belonging to GOD.

"On the other hand in Apoc. xii. 11, *they overcame him because of the blood of the Lamb*, Apoc. vii. 14, *they washed their robes, and made them white in the blood of the Lamb*, 1 John i. 7, *the blood of Jesus his Son cleanseth us from all sin*, the conception of the Blood as an energetic power, as a fountain of life, opened by death and flowing still, is clearly marked.

"This latter thought explains the stress which St John lays on the issue of the blood and the water from the side of the Lord after the Crucifixion (John xix. 34; 1 John v. 6 ff.). That which was outwardly, physically, death, was yet reconcileable with life. Christ lived even in Death and through Death.

"In the Epistle to the Hebrews the manifold efficacy of Christ's Blood is directly illustrated by a parallel with two representative sacrifices, the Cove-

NOTE VIII. nant Sacrifice by which Israel was brought into fellowship with God (Hebr. ix. 15 ff.), and the Service of the Day of Atonement, by which the broken fellowship was again restored (Hebr. ix. 11 ff.).

"The Blood of Christ is the Blood of the New Covenant: Hebr. ix. 15 ff. Comp. Matt. xxvi. 28; Mk. xiv. 34; Lc. xxii. 20, 1 Cor. xi. 25, 27 (cp. 1 Cor. x. 16); and it is the Blood through which He as our High Priest enters into the Presence of God for us: Hebr. ix. 12, 23 ff.; comp. xiii. 12, i. 3. These two aspects of the truth need to be carefully regarded. By 'sprinkling' of Christ's Blood the believer is first brought into fellowship with God in Christ; and in the imperfect conduct of his personal life, the life of Christ is continually communicated to him for growth and cleansing. He himself enters into the Divine Presence 'in the Blood of Jesus' (Hebr. x. 19) surrounded, as it were, and supported by the Life which flows from Him.

"Similar thoughts find expression in the other writings of the New Testament. Thus we read with predominant reference to the initial act of salvation:

Acts xx. 28. *The church of GOD, which he purchased with his own blood.*

1 Pet. i. 18 f. *Ye were redeemed...with precious blood, as of a lamb without blemish and without spot, even the blood of Christ.*

Col. i. 20. *Having made peace through the blood of his cross.*

"But even in such cases the first act is not regarded as an isolated act of forgiveness. It is the beginning of a state which continues: NOTE VIII.

Much more then, being now justified by his blood, shall we be saved from the wrath of GOD through him. Rom. v. 9.

In whom we have our redemption through his blood, the forgiveness of our trespasses, according to the riches of his grace. Eph. i. 7.

But now in Christ Jesus ye that once were far off are made nigh in the blood of Christ. Eph. ii. 13.

"In other places the thought of the continuous efficacy of Christ's Blood as a power of life is even more conspicuous:

To the elect...unto obedience and sprinkling of the blood of Jesus Christ. 1 Pet. i. 1, 2.

How much more shall the blood of Christ, who through the eternal Spirit offered himself without blemish unto GOD, cleanse your conscience from dead works to serve the living GOD? Hebr. x. 14.

Having therefore, brethren, boldness to enter into the holy place in the blood of Jesus, by the way which he dedicated for us, a new and living way... Hebr. x. 19 f.

(*Ye are come nigh*) *to Jesus the mediator of a new covenant, and to the blood of sprinkling that speaketh better than that of Abel.* Hebr. xii. 24.

"The two elements which are thus included in the thought of Christ's Blood, or, in the narrower sense of the word, of Christ's Death and Christ's Blood, that is of Christ's Death (the Blood shed) and of Christ's Life (the Blood offered) are indicated

NOTE VIII. clearly in [*God*] *is faithful and righteous to for-*
1 John i. 9. *give us our sins* (the virtue of Christ's Death); *and to cleanse us from all unrighteousness* (the virtue of Christ's Life)[1]."

[1] Additional note on 1 John i. 7. Compare also a very suggestive note of Prof. Milligan, *The Resurrection of the Lord*, pp. 263 ff.

NOTE IX.

THE COMMUNION OF SAINTS[1].

[1] This paper was read at the Church Congress of Leicester in 1880. In answer to many requests to reprint it, I have ventured to place it here as giving some of the thoughts which I have been anxious to suggest in a practical form. A commemoration of Benefactors was commenced at Peterborough Cathedral in 1881.

Ye are all one man in Christ Jesus.

GAL. iii. 28.

There is one body and one Spirit.

EPH. iv. 4.

I. THE idea of a communion of saints includes two main thoughts—the thought of a life wider than the life of sense; and the thought of a life under conditions different from those of earth. The communion is a communion of saints as saints, and not as men under the present conditions of humanity. It is independent of limitations of time and space, both in its range and in its fulfilment. Each thought is of the highest practical importance. NOTE IX.

1. Of the many great conceptions which are characteristic of our generation—voices of GOD, as I believe, calling us to unregarded truths in His Word—no one is more characteristic than that of the dependence of man on man as well as on nature. We are learning, by the help of many teachers, the extent and the authority of the dominion which the dead exercise over us, and which we ourselves are shaping for our descendants. We feel, as perhaps it was impossible to feel before, how at every moment influences from the past enter our souls, and how we in turn scatter abroad that which will be fruitful in

NOTE IX. the distant future. It is becoming clear to us that we are literally parts of others and they of us.

Dependence is, indeed, an inexorable law of natural life. Our faith has anticipated the conclusion and hallowed it. Men must be dependent on one another. For saints this dependence is transfigured into fellowship. The believer recognises that the power which acts upon him from without is the expression of a spiritual life. He sees that the image of Christ's Body gives the truest possible view of the relation in which all who are 'in Him' stand to one another. The one life, the one Spirit, by which they are united to their Head, united eternally, unites them now, in time, to one another. In that divine vision life appears in the fullest proportions we can yet apprehend. We turn from the living to the dead, and, as we contemplate the splendour of the heritage which they have bequeathed to us, we confess with no unworthy self-disparagement that without them we are incomplete. We turn from the dead to the living, and as we trace the lineaments of a divine likeness in those about us, we give thanks without presumption that there are saints now.

2. Again, this vast life which reaches through all time is in its nature beyond time. We are constrained, in our attempts to give distinctness to it, to use the language of earth, but in itself the spiritual life, of which the Communion of Saints is the foretaste, belongs to another order. And, however hard

it may be to pierce the veil of phenomena, this is what our faith claims of us to aim at. Our efforts, in other words, must be directed not to materializing heaven, but to discerning the divine, the eternal, in earth. As it is, we too often communicate our own deadness to the creation, which is waiting for the manifestation of the Sons of GOD; and rest when we are bidden to enter the unseen. Yet we do not doubt in theory that we are immortal beings moving among the works of GOD, accomplishing His purposes, ministering to His glory; and if the life which angels contemplate with eager desire is poor to us, it is only because we allow our eyes to be satisfied with the surface. NOTE IX.

The teaching of Scripture guards us against this perilous blindness. The words of the Lord and of His Apostles assure us that eternal life is here. Our blessings and our struggles lie now 'in the heavenly realm' (ἐν τοῖς ἐπουρανίοις). 'Our life hath been hid in GOD.' 'We have come to a heavenly Jerusalem, to an innumerable company of angels, to the general assembly and church of the first-born.' The communion of saints in the largest sense, the communion of angels and men, of men already perfected, and of men struggling towards the crown which is prepared for them, is a present reality. There is one divine kingdom, and there are many worlds. There is one life which finds expression in many forms, but that life is greater, deeper than all.

NOTE IX. II. How, then, can we realise it? The answer will naturally take account of the two sides of man's life. Each believer has his individual character, which must be hallowed as though he were alone; and he brings this to the service of the whole body of which he is a part. The communion of saints must, therefore, be realised socially and personally—socially, to speak briefly, by commemoration, personally by meditation.

1. But here as elsewhere the social life is the true starting point of the personal life. We turn then first to public commemoration as furnishing the occasion through which individual fellowship with the spiritual world is quickened and guided. And in this respect no one can fail to have felt how imperfectly our Kalendar reflects the divine history of the Church. We must ask when we look upon it whether we do indeed believe in the continuous manifestation of the Spirit, and claim descent from an ancestry of saints. The Apostolic age stands there without preparation and without sequel. The old dispensation finds no representative from among the heroes of faith, lawgiver, or prince, or prophet, Enoch or Elijah, Moses or David, Samuel or Isaiah. The new dispensation finds no representative from among those, who in Christ's name and by Christ's power brought modern life and thought into His service. A few names, a few events, indeed, which witness to an effort after a larger sympathy, still

keep a place in it; but even these cease with Hugh of Lincoln and Richard of Chichester, before our own Church entered on its characteristic work in the old world or in the new. NOTE IX.

As a necessary consequence of this narrow range of the commemoration of saints among us, our type of saintship has been dwarfed and impoverished; it has been removed far from the stir and conflicts of ordinary action. The kingly type and the prophetic type, the type of the artist and of the poet and of the scholar, have been put aside. We do not turn to those by whom these characters have been fulfilled in Christ's strength as the peers of martyrs and apostles. We do not seek in their examples the pledge of the consecration of gifts similar, however small, among ourselves.

And yet we cannot afford to dispense with the widest teaching of consecrated lives. We daily lose much by not placing these in their right position in the open teaching of the Church.

It is true, indeed, that every type of essential human excellence coexists in Christ, the Son of Man; but we, 'who are but parts, can see but part—now this, now that.' We have no power to apprehend directly elements which are combined with others in an absolute ideal. It is only through Christ's servants each realising, according to his nature, his endowments, his age, his country, some feature in the Christly life that we come to have a real sense of the fulness of

NOTE IX. His Humanity. The many typical characters who foreshadowed Him find their counterpart in the many saints who offer for our welcome and our study the riches of His manhood. Nor do they in the least degree trench upon His inviolable honour. Their saintliness is wholly from Him. They are what they are, so far as we call them to mind and seek their fellowship, by His presence, He in them and they in Him. They have made His power visible; and for this we are bound to commemorate them, and their Lord through them.

The neglect or the indifference of centuries, no less than the discordances which are found in every life, involves such commemoration in great difficulties. Yet our faith encourages us to face them; and in many cases the solution will come through obvious channels. There are few parishes which do not include in their annals some names fitted to recall memories of Christ's manifold victories through believers. A dedication festival may not unfrequently lay open a fruitful page of Christian work. Our Cathedrals, again, are monuments of sacrifice and service which constrain us to recall Christ's working through those whose benefactions we inherit. Most of us, I fancy, have been deeply stirred by the commemoration services of College and University. We have wondered, perhaps, that the use is not universal. At Peterborough, in old time, to take one instance, almost every abbot had his memorial day, and four times in the year, in the Ember weeks, all were commemorated together. There is surely here something for us to embody under new forms of thought. NOTE IX.

I should be the last to forget or to disparage the services of unknown benefactors. These have in a large degree made life for us what it is. These have their own commemoration when we recall the progress of the ages. But there are others who stand out as leaders, as representatives. Gifts, labours, thoughts of distinguishable ancestors go to swell our spiritual patrimony. It may have been by some conspicuous work which was nobly spread over a lifetime: it may have been by some sweet trait which was just seen in a crisis of trial; but 'here and here' they have helped us, and if we are to enjoy the fulness of their service we must solemnly recall it. In doing this we arrogate to ourselves no authority of final judgment by grateful celebration. We recognise a blessing; and, so far, we acknowledge God's love in him by whose ministry it was shewn to us. Nor would it, I think, be difficult to make a list of names from our own Church which all would accept as worthy of memory, names of rulers and scholars, of men who taught by their words and by their lives, who spread the faith and deepened our knowledge of it.

Such commemoration of men, such peopling with familiar forms of the vacancies of All Saints' Day, such filling up the noble but blank outlines of the *Te Deum*, would help us to understand better, as a

NOTE IX. society, the vastness of the Christian life; but we require also the commemoration of ideas (if I may so speak) in order that we may bear in mind the new conditions of the spiritual life, which, as we have seen, are suggested by the belief in the Communion of Saints. And here one festival still survives by name in our Kalendar which completely expresses part of what I mean, the Festival of the Transfiguration. The Transfiguration is the revelation of the potential spirituality of the earthly life in the highest outward form. In that the present and the past are seen in a fellowship of glory; and the future in its great features lies open for consideration. Such an event, distinct in its teaching from the Resurrection, and yet closely akin to it, calls for more religious recognition than it receives. It is able, if we enter into its meaning, to bring vividly before us the reality of a communion of the living and the dead. Here, as elsewhere, the Lord, as the Son of Man, gives the measure of the capacity of humanity, and shews that to which He leads those who are united with Him.

The festival of the Transfiguration furnishes an opportunity for bringing out the idea of the widest fellowship of men. The festival of St Michael and All Angels furnishes an opportunity for bringing out the complementary idea of the interpenetration of human life by life of another order. And if it be true (and who has not felt it?) that 'the world'—the world of sense—'is too much with us,' then a remedy is here offered for our use. The reserve and the revelations of Scripture are equally eloquent. I will notice one point only, which seems to be practically overlooked. We commonly limit our notion of angelic service to personal ministration. No doubt Scripture dwells specially on this kind of office; but it indicates yet more, a ministration of angels in nature, which brings both them and the world closer to men. There is, I venture to think, something in this aspect of our subject worthy of attention. Perhaps one effect of the growing clearness with which we apprehend the laws of physical phenomena is to bring out into prominence the thought of the powers which work according to them. The sense of action by law places the agent very near to us. 'I can see,' writes one who was himself a distinguished physiologist, 'nothing in all nature but the loving acts of spiritual beings.' However strange the conception may be, it contains, I believe, truths which we have not yet mastered. And in this respect we commonly embarrass ourselves by mentally presenting all action under the forms of human action. Spirit, it is obvious, may act in other ways; and our festival of the heavenly order remains to help us little by little to apprehend in this larger sense the revelation of the Communion of Saints.

2. So far we have seen how public commemoration can supply examples and thoughts towards realising the Communion of Saints. These are made effective personally by meditation. And, to our great

NOTE IX. loss, the faculty and the habit of meditation have not as yet been cultivated among us. Our national character, and, at present, the prevailing spirit of realism are alien from it. Yet the praise to GOD's glory which comes through the devout consideration of His action in men is true work. This is a subject for spiritual meditation; and periods of quiet retirement may be made available for pursuing it.

But, as it is, we are apt to dwell on the littlenesses of men, or if not, upon the picturesque aspects of their lives, to bring them down in some measure to our level, and not to aspire to their highest.

It is, however, through such aspiration alone, quickened by the thoughtful study of that which the Spirit wrought in them, that we can enter into fellowship with their true life. Weaknesses, faults, errors, accidents of time and place, fall away. We learn to look upon the love, the courage, the faith, the self-sacrifice, the simplicity of truth which they embodied, and so become invigorated by vital contact with the eternal manifested through men. We rise, so far as we can rise under the pressure of earthly limitations, to some perception of the heavenly life, in which all that is personal is gathered up without the loss of personality in One, even 'in Christ.'

This fellowship of spirit with spirit is closer, and may be more powerful, than the precious fellowship which we can hold with books. That leads to this. The record of a life imaged in word and deed, the energy of a life shewn in thoughts grasped and made ready for use, help to gain an energetic sympathy with those who have laboured and written for the truth. NOTE IX.

And there is no limit to this inspiring communion. It embraces the living and the dead. It acknowledges no saddest necessity of outward separation as reaching to the region in which it is. It does not even seek for the confirmation of any visible pledge. It makes possible that unity of inward love to which final conquest is promised. It rests on that which is the source of action. It imparts to the believer something of the strength of every victory of faith. For by saints we understand all who welcome and appropriate and shew forth, in whatever way, the gifts of the Spirit. We look to the one life, flowing from the One Paraclete, and, by tracing the manifoldness of His action, gain strength for our own task.

In this case also special circumstances will serve to determine the peculiar objects of our meditation. Our position, our duties, our temptations, our endowments, will influence our choice. If we are ready to follow, Christ, through the Spirit sent in His name, will guide us to some one in whom we may study the virtue of His presence.

And in this connexion I cannot forbear to notice the possible influence of what we speak of, with too little reflection, as Christian names. They are indeed, and they can be treated as, the dedication names of each believer.

NOTE IX. Meditation on the saintliness of saintly men must be supplemented by meditation on angels, as the representatives of the unseen world, if we are to feel the full extent of the Communion of Saints. We cannot, it is true, presume to press such meditations into detail. It is enough if we recognise the service, the sympathy of 'the host of heaven'; if we consider all that is implied in the most familiar and solemn words by which we claim to share their hymns of divine praise in our highest act of thanksgiving and communion.

III. Briefly, then, to sum up in another form what has been said, we must, as far as we may be able, both in public service and in private thought, present and dwell upon the greatest facts, the greatest aspects of things, the greatest truths, refusing to rest on the transitory and temporal, if we are to realise, as we can do, the Communion of Saints, the fulness of the manifestation of the spiritual life, and its eternal power.

The familiar example of hymns will shew beyond question what a capacity there is in this treatment of our faith, without any suppression of individual convictions, to unite, to elevate, to inspire, by unseen forces, those who are kept apart by intellectual and material obstacles. A hymn-book is a confession of the Communion of Saints.

Nor can we forget that the charge to strive after

the fulfilment of this article of our Creed is laid specially upon us. It is peculiar to the Western Creed, and it dates from an era of transition[1]. The recollection of the old Empire, the anticipation of a new Empire, stirred the souls of men in the eighth century to proclaim a personal force of undying life in the spiritual society. It was not enough for them to acknowledge their belief in a Holy Catholic Church as a great fact: they felt that it must be a source of power; and that conviction they have handed down to us that we may realise it now, when some aspects of the continuity and solidarity of life have been made more evident than in earlier times. Modern science has given us forms which we can animate. NOTE IX.

There is, indeed, a danger as well as a use in the contemplation of great ideals. If they lift us for a while above the strife of details, they may unfit us for dealing with the concrete questions which arise in daily work. But this ideal of one spiritual life, seen in its many parts through the ages and everywhere around us, made our own by the Communion of Saints, seems to me to be most practical in its influence. The one ground of union is the possession of a common life, and not any nicely calculated scheme of compromise. To see the life even from afar, to look towards it, is in some degree to reach a serener atmosphere, to feel

[1] The article first appeared in the Creed of Faustus of Riez towards the end of the fifth century and gained general acceptance in the eighth.

NOTE IX. the true proportion of things, to gain the earnest of an interpretation of the mysteries by which we are perplexed.

This thought of a life eternal, underlying, so to speak, the fleeting phenomena of sense, not future so much as shrouded, is characteristic of Christianity; it is included in the fact of the Incarnation, and it meets our present distress and disharmony with a message of hope. I say 'our present distress'; for do we not all sorrowfully admit that the elements of our being are unreconciled, that there is on all sides a strenuous occupation with the outside of things which tends to destroy real reverence; that even the highest religious faculties are engaged or distracted by external details? To such discordance and unrest and triviality the sense of a present fellowship in an existence infinite in its variety, one in its essence, divine in its spring and issue, brings the appropriate and adequate help.

Man is made to seek for the rest which it provides. Most of those who hear me will remember the magnificent myth in the *Phædrus*, in which Plato seeks to explain the origin of the highest forces in our earthly being. On stated days human souls, he says, follow in the train of the gods, and rising above the world gaze on the eternal and the absolute. It is only by strenuous and painful endeavour that they can gain for a brief space the vision, which is the appointed food of diviner natures. Then they fall to earth, and their bodily life corresponds with the range and clearness of the celestial impressions which they retain. So they recognise about them during their earthly sojourn the images of higher things, and again strive upwards. NOTE IX.

For us the revelation of Christ has made this dream a truth. In Him we see perfect sacrifice, perfect truth, perfect wisdom, perfect love; and having seen it we can discern signs of His Presence in them who shew His gifts. He gives unity, and they reveal to us His fulness. In our kinsmanship with them we welcome the pledge of a life which is beyond time. Meanwhile, it is a blessing to acknowledge, once and again, a spiritual master. We grow stronger by the devotion of loyal discipleship. We 'see the light and whence it flows,' the light which is life eternal; and the Communion of Saints, with its manifold supplies of strength, with its boundless wealth of promise, becomes a fact of immediate experience.

WORTHY ART THOU, OUR LORD AND OUR GOD, TO RECEIVE THE GLORY AND THE HONOUR AND THE POWER: FOR THOU DIDST CREATE ALL THINGS, AND BECAUSE OF THY WILL THEY WERE, AND WERE CREATED.

CAMBRIDGE: PRINTED BY J. AND C. F. CLAY, AT THE UNIVERSITY PRESS.